treat petites

treat petites

TINY SWEETS ❧ AND ❧ SAVORY PLEASURES

Fiona Pearce

STERLING EPICURE
New York

STERLING EPICURE
New York

An Imprint of Sterling Publishing
387 Park Avenue South
New York, NY 10016

This 2014 edition published by Sterling Epicure by arrangement with
Ivy Press Ltd.

This book was conceived, designed, and produced by

Ivy Press

Creative Director Peter Bridgewater
Publisher Susan Kelly
Conceived by Sophie Collins
Editorial Director Tom Kitch
Art Director Wayne Blades
Design & art direction Simon Daley
Photography Sian Irvine & Clive Streeter

ISBN 978-1-4549-1067-1

Distributed in Canada by Sterling Publishing
c/o Canadian Manda Group, 165 Dufferin Street
Toronto, Ontario, Canada M6K 3H6

For information about custom editions, special sales, and premium and
corporate purchases, please contact Sterling Special Sales at 800-805-5489
or specialsales@sterlingpublishing.com.

Manufactured in China

Color origination by Ivy Press Reprographics

2 4 6 8 10 9 7 5 3 1

www.sterlingpublishing.com

· This book uses both metric and imperial measurements.
Follow the same units of measurements throughout; do not mix
metric and imperial.

· All spoon measurements are level. Teaspoons are
assumed to be 5 ml and tablespoons 15 ml.

· Unless otherwise stated, milk is assumed to be whole, eggs are
extra-large, and individual fruits and vegetables are medium.

Contents

There's an *Alice in Wonderland* charm about teeny chocolate éclairs, delectable miniature Victoria sponge cakes, buttonlike macarons … any little treats you can just pop in your mouth and finish in a bite. It's no surprise that bite-size versions of popular bakes and desserts are the latest trend sweeping Parisian patisseries and New York bakeries. Not only are mini desserts supercute, you can enjoy them while keeping your indulgence in check!

Each chapter of this book is full of seriously adorable and delectable tiny bakes that you can easily re-create at home. Whether you prefer making lovely little sweet treats to serve at an afternoon party, or mouth-watering hors d'oeuvre to impress guests at a cocktail party, there are 42 different recipes to choose from. All the recipes can be prepared without a lot of special equipment, and each chapter features some useful baking tips to help you achieve a professional finish. Basic recipes for the foundation of some popular bakes, such as meringue and pastry dough, are also included so that you can use them as a blank canvas to create your own miniature delights.

Basic Tools & Equipment

You really don't need a lot of fancy kitchen gadgets to create miniature treats, but there are a few pieces of equipment that are useful to have on hand to make baking easier and to help you achieve professional-looking results:

Pastry cutters

Small round pastry cutters (up to 2 inches/5 cm in diameter) are useful for cutting out little pieces of sponge cake, tiny cookies, and pastry circles to make canapés or galettes.

Cookie cutters

Small metal cookie cutters in a range of shapes can be useful for cutting out treats. There are many cutter shapes available and you can easily adapt cookie designs to make them seasonal.

Tartlet pans

Individual mini tartlet pans, 1–2 inches (2.5 cm–5 cm) in diameter, are incredibly cute and are essential for making bite-size tartlets.

Pastry bags

Disposable and reusable pastry bags can be fitted with piping tips for piping frostings, fillings, and choux pastry.

Piping tips

Piping tips can be used to pipe meringues, fillings, or frostings, or to pipe dainty choux pastry shapes. Small round or star piping tips (no bigger than ½ inch/1 cm in diameter) are used in this book.

Squeeze bottles

These bottles are useful for making blinis or mini pancakes—they enable you to squeeze out the exact amount of liquid mixture you need. They can also be filled with thinned royal icing to flood cookies.

Baking sheets

Lined with parchment paper, baking sheets are essential for any bakes.

Mini baking pans

There are many baking pans available in different shapes, and they vary in size and capacity. Mini madeleine pans and mini cupcake pans are used to create some of the recipes in this book.

Paintbrushes or mini pastry brushes

These are used for applying egg wash to pastry dough before baking and for dusting treats with edible luster dust and edible gold leaf.

Nonstick rolling pin

This is an essential tool for rolling out pie and cookie dough.

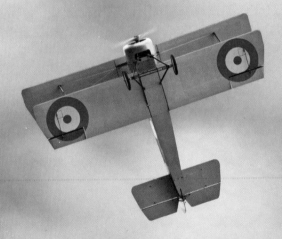

Sponges

Sponges

Sponge cakes can form a fundamental building block in your baking repertoire. If you have a regular baked sponge on hand, a wide range of lovely miniature treats is only steps away.

Vanilla Sponge Cake

This recipe involves minimal preparation and produces a light, fluffy vanilla sponge.

Makes two 8-inch/20-cm round, or two 7-inch/18-cm square, or two 12-inch x 8-inch (30-cm x 20-cm) rectangular jellyroll pans

2 sticks (225 g) butter, softened, plus extra for greasing
1 cup (200 g) + 2 tbsp superfine sugar
4 extra-large eggs
scant 1⅔ cups (225 g) all-purpose flour
3½ tsp baking powder
1 tsp vanilla extract

Preheat the oven to 350°F/180°C. Grease the sides and bottom of two baking pans and line the bottoms with parchment paper.

Using an electric mixer, beat all the ingredients together on medium speed until well blended.

Spoon the batter into the prepared pans and spread evenly with a spatula.

Bake in the preheated oven for 25 minutes (or about 15 minutes for jellyroll pans), or until well risen and a toothpick inserted into the center comes out clean.

Let the sponge cakes cool in the pans for 5 minutes before turning them out onto a wire rack to cool completely.

TIPS

Sift the flour twice to aerate it and remove any lumps. This helps create a light sponge.

Avoid taking a sneaky peek at the cake halfway through the baking time—a sudden rush of cool air entering the oven will cause the cake to sink.

ADDING FLAVOR

You can choose from a variety of flavors to add to your Vanilla Sponge Cake batter:
Lemon Add the finely grated zest and juice of ½ an unwaxed lemon. There is also a wide range of lemon oils that you can add instead.
Chocolate Replace ½ cup (70 g) of the all-purpose flour with sifted unsweetened cocoa powder.
Coffee Add 3 tbsp cooled espresso or strongly brewed black coffee.

Vanilla Buttercream

Make your sponge cakes truly memorable with just a few swipes of your spatula. A simple buttercream recipe is all you need to start with, then add a flavoring or coloring to tailor your cakes to any occasion.

1½ sticks (175 g) unsalted butter, softened
3 cups (350 g) confectioners' sugar, sifted
2 tbsp cooled boiled water
1 tsp vanilla extract

Using an electric mixer, beat all the ingredients together for at least 5 minutes, until the mixture is light and fluffy. It is best to start mixing on a slow speed to prevent the confectioners' sugar from covering the kitchen, and then gradually build up to a fast speed.

TIP

Cover the mixing bowl with a damp, clean dish cloth while mixing the buttercream to stop the confectioners' sugar from escaping.

Miniature Layer Cakes

Best known in Britain as a "Victoria sandwich" and first noted by the redoubtable Mrs. Beeton in her *The Book of Household Management* published in 1861, this delicious sponge cake has the finest provenance and has been a favorite on tables all over the world ever since. Well risen, light, and subtly flavored with vanilla, these minis, like their big sister, are simply filled with whipped cream, raspberry and rose water preserve, and a little fresh fruit.

To make 24

1 To make the preserve, preheat the oven to 300°F/150°C and place a saucer in the refrigerator to chill. Place the sugar on a baking sheet lined with parchment paper and put it in the oven for 10 minutes to warm.

2 Meanwhile, put the raspberries in a saucepan and heat slowly, then bring them to a boil for 5 minutes. Remove the pan from the heat and add the warmed sugar and rose water. Stir the mixture over low heat until the sugar has dissolved. Bring the mixture back to a boil and let boil for about 10 minutes, until setting point is reached. You can test that you have reached this point by spooning a little of the preserve onto the chilled saucer, letting it cool for a few minutes, and then pushing your finger into it. If it wrinkles, it is ready; if not, return the pan to the heat and cook for an additional minute or two and test again.

3 When the preserve has reached setting point, carefully ladle it into sterilized screw-top jars, leaving a ½-inch/1-cm gap at the top, and twist the lids on while the preserve is still hot. The preserve will thicken as it cools. Store it in the refrigerator and use within a couple of weeks.

4 To make the filling, whip the cream with the sugar and vanilla extract in a bowl until it holds its shape.

5 To assemble the sponge cakes, use a 1½–2-inch/4–5-cm round cutter to cut out 48 circles of sponge. Spread a thin layer of preserve on half the quantity of circles, then spoon a little of the whipped cream on top. Spread the chopped raspberries on top of the cream and then place another sponge circle on top. Lightly dust the tops of the cakes with confectioners' sugar before serving.

2 Vanilla Sponge Cakes, each baked in a 12-inch x 8-inch (30-cm x 20-cm) jellyroll pan (*see page 13*)

RASPBERRY & ROSE WATER PRESERVE

3 cups (600 g) granulated sugar

4 cups (500 g) fresh raspberries, rinsed and drained

2 tsp rose water

FILLING

1¼ cups (300 ml) heavy cream

1 tbsp confectioners' sugar, plus extra for dusting

½ tsp vanilla extract

generous ¾ cup (100 g) fresh raspberries, chopped into quarters

ACTUAL SIZE

Iced Cakes

Coated with shiny icing in pink and lavender, and finished with minute chocolate motifs, only the finest bone china tea service will match the delicacy of these delightful sponge cakes. And they taste as good as they look.

To make 64

8-inch (20-cm) square Vanilla Sponge Cake (*see page 13*)

1 quantity of Vanilla Buttercream (*see page 13*)

4 tbsp apricot preserve, warmed

10½ oz (300 g) marzipan

3½ oz (100 g) semisweet chocolate, melted, for decorating (optional)

ICING

6 cups (750 g) confectioners' sugar, sifted

½ cup (125 ml) water

2 tbsp light corn syrup

1 tsp vanilla extract (or other flavoring, if desired)

pink and baby blue food coloring

ACTUAL SIZE

1 Slice the sponge in half horizontally. Wrap and freeze one half. Carefully slice the remaining cake in half horizontally again to create two layers of cake, each about ½ inch (1 cm) thick. Spread a thin layer of the buttercream over the bottom sponge layer, using a spatula. Place the other half of the sponge on top of the buttercream. Brush the top and sides of the sponge cake with the warmed preserve, using a pastry brush.

2 Using a nonstick rolling pin, roll out the marzipan into a square about ⅛ inch (3 mm) thick, then place it on top of the cake and gently press it down with the palm of your hand or a cake smoother to make sure that it sticks firmly to the cake. Use a knife to trim the marzipan so that it doesn't hang over the edge of the cake. Score 1-inch (2.5-cm) squares into the marzipan with a sharp knife. Place the sponge in the refrigerator for at least an hour, until firm.

3 Meanwhile, make the icing by combining the sugar, water, corn syrup, and vanilla extract in a saucepan, and stir the mixture continuously over low heat. Place a candy thermometer into the mixture. At 91°F/33°C, the icing should be a pouring consistency but not too thin. Carefully increase the temperature to 113–122°F/45–50°C. Remove the thermometer—if the icing sets hard on the tip of it within seconds the icing is ready. Remove the saucepan from the heat and stir in 2–3 drops of pink food coloring.

4 Remove the sponge from the refrigerator and cut it into 1-inch (2.5-cm) squares, using the scored lines as a guide. Sit each sponge square in turn on a fork held over the bowl of icing, then use a spoon to pour the warm icing over the square, allowing any excess icing to drip back into the bowl. If desired, cover half the quantity of squares with pink icing, then mix some baby blue food coloring into the pink icing to tint it to a lavender color and cover the remaining squares with the lavender icing. Place the squares on a wire rack to dry before putting them into petit four/mini paper cake liners. Store the cakes in an airtight container for up to 3 days.

EXTRA If desired, make small chocolate motifs by pouring melted semisweet chocolate into a silicone mold and letting it set. Flex the mold to remove the chocolate motifs and then place one on top of each cake before the icing has set.

Earl Grey Madeleines with Honey-Orange Glaze

You can bake these classics in any miniature pans, but to get the distinctive fluted shape, find a mini madeleine pan online or in your local cook store. Bite through the crisp honey glaze into the light tea-flavored sponge and you'll find yourself transported, with Proustian accuracy, straight to a French sidewalk café …

To make 48

1 Grind the tea leaves into a fine powder using a mortar and pestle, then rub the sugar into the ground tea leaves with your fingertips.

2 Using an electric mixer, beat the eggs and tea-flavored sugar together until the mixture is creamy and has doubled in size. Slowly fold in the flour, baking powder, and salt until well combined. Add the vanilla extract and then gently stir in the melted butter. Cover the batter with plastic wrap and chill in the refrigerator for at least 2 hours. This allows the gluten to relax, giving the madeleines a light texture when they are baked.

3 Preheat the oven to 350°F/180°C. Brush a mini madeleine baking pan with melted butter.

4 Spoon about 1 teaspoonful of the cake batter into each section of the baking pan to fill them two-thirds full. (Keep any remaining cake batter refrigerated until ready to bake.) Chill the filled baking pan in the refrigerator for 10 minutes before baking in the preheated oven for 4 minutes, or until the madeleines have risen and begin to shrink away from the edges of the pan. (Keep any remaining cake batter refrigerated until ready to bake.) Turn the madeleines out onto a wire rack to cool completely.

5 To make the glaze, mix the sugar, honey, and orange juice together in a bowl with a spoon. Sprinkle in the orange zest and stir until combined. Once all the cakes have cooled, gently dip into the glaze, sprinkle with more orange zest, and lay them on parchment paper to dry before serving.

3 tbsp loose Earl Grey tea
½ cup (100 g) superfine sugar
2 extra-large eggs
¾ cup (100 g) all-purpose flour
½ tsp baking powder
pinch of salt
1 tsp vanilla extract
5 tbsp (75 g) unsalted butter, melted and cooled, plus extra for greasing

HONEY-ORANGE GLAZE

½ cup (60 g) confectioners' sugar, sifted
1 tsp honey
2 tbsp fresh orange juice
1 tsp finely grated unwaxed orange zest, plus extra for sprinkling

ACTUAL SIZE

Chocolate Celebration Cakes

Light but rich, génoise sponge is a good choice for a layer cake. These featherlight miniatures are cut from a thin sheet of cake, then layered and topped with a strawberry buttercream, piped with a star piping tip to give an elegant swirled finish. Sugar roses add a suitably genteel finishing touch.

To make 8

⅓ cup (50 g) all-purpose flour

⅓ cup (35 g) unsweetened cocoa powder

4 extra-large eggs

½ cup (100 g) superfine sugar

3½ tbsp (50 g) butter, melted and hot, plus extra for greasing

sugar flowers or sprinkles, for decorating

STRAWBERRY BUTTERCREAM

2 tbsp strawberry preserve or jelly (homemade or store-bought)

1 quantity of Vanilla Buttercream (*see page 13*)

pink food coloring (optional)

ACTUAL SIZE

1 To make the strawberry buttercream, stir the preserve or jelly through the buttercream until it is well incorporated. If desired, stir in a drop of pink food coloring to make the buttercream a brighter pink color. Spoon it into a pastry bag fitted with a small star piping tip and set aside.

2 To make the chocolate génoise sponge, preheat the oven to 325°F/160°C. Grease a 8-inch (20-cm) square baking pan and line the bottom with parchment paper. Sift the flour and cocoa powder together three times and set aside. Place the eggs in a large heatproof bowl and whisk in the sugar until combined. Set the bowl over a small saucepan of simmering water over medium-low heat and whisk the mixture constantly until it is warm and foamy.

3 Remove the bowl from the pan and then beat it with a handheld electric mixer on high speed until the bubbles start to disappear and the mixture triples in volume. Reduce the mixing speed and beat for an additional minute. This will help to stabilize the air bubbles in the cake batter.

4 Sift half the flour mixture into the bowl and gently fold it in until almost fully combined. Sift in the remaining flour mixture and fold in until well combined, but be careful not to overmix.

5 Add one-third of the cake batter to the hot melted butter in a separate bowl. Use a small spatula to fold the butter thoroughly into the cake batter. Pour this back into the bulk of the cake batter and fold in gently. Spoon the cake batter into the prepared baking pan. Tilt the pan so that the batter spreads out evenly and drop it two to three times on the counter to burst the air bubbles.

6 Bake in the preheated oven for 15–20 minutes, until the cake springs back when touched gently and a toothpick inserted into the center comes out clean. Let the cake cool completely in the pan.

7 To assemble the cakes, use a 1½-inch/4-cm round cutter to cut out 16 circles of sponge cake. Pipe buttercream on top of half the quantity of sponge circles, then place another sponge circle on top. Pipe a swirl of buttercream on the top of each cake, then adorn with decorations of your own choice, such as sugar flowers or sprinkles.

Lemon Domes with Pink Grapefruit Syrup

Fancy domed molds shape a batch of delicate lemon sponge cakes, which are soaked in sweet grapefruit and lemon syrup after baking. They are best served in canapé spoons, or in tiny bowls along with a teaspoon so that you can scoop up the last delicious drops.

1 Preheat the oven to 350°F/180°C. Grease 24 mini brioche molds generously and place them on a baking sheet. Using an electric mixer, beat the butter and sugar together until light and fluffy. Gradually beat in the egg until it is well combined. Sift in the flour and baking powder, then gently fold in the lemon and grapefruit zest.

2 Divide the batter between the prepared mini molds, then bake in the preheated oven for about 15 minutes, until golden and the cake springs back when lightly pressed. Let the cakes cool for 5 minutes in their molds and then turn them out onto a wire rack to cool completely.

3 To make the syrup, use a vegetable peeler to peel strips of rind from the lemon and grapefruit. Use a small knife to remove as much pith as possible from the rinds. Tear the rinds into thin strips and then blanch them in boiling water before combining them in a saucepan with the lemon juice, grapefruit juice, and sugar. Bring the syrup to a boil and continue to cook over high heat for about 2 minutes, or until the rinds become translucent. Let the syrup cool before drizzling it over the cakes. If desired, sprinkle the tops of the cakes with fine strips of lemon and grapefruit zest to decorate before serving.

To make 24

4 tbsp (55 g) unsalted butter, softened, plus extra for greasing

⅓ cup (60 g) superfine sugar

1 extra-large egg

generous ⅓ cup (60 g) all-purpose flour

1½ tsp baking powder

finely grated zest of 1 unwaxed lemon

finely grated zest of 1 unwaxed pink grapefruit

PINK GRAPEFRUIT SYRUP

1 unwaxed lemon

½ unwaxed pink grapefruit

5 tbsp fresh lemon juice

5 tbsp fresh pink grapefruit juice

1 cup (200 g) superfine sugar

fine strips of unwaxed lemon and pink grapefruit zest, for decorating (optional)

ACTUAL SIZE

Meringues

Meringues

A meringue is an airy mixture of stiffly beaten egg whites and sugar. Most people associate meringue with light, billowy peaks atop a classic lemon meringue pie, but it can also be piped with a pastry bag into attractive shapes and baked to a sweet, crisp cloud to cradle delicious toppings.

Meringue Mixture

3½ oz (100 g) egg whites (3 large egg whites)
½ cup (100 g) superfine sugar
1 tsp vanilla extract
scant 1 cup (100 g) confectioners' sugar, sifted

Using an electric mixer, start beating the egg whites on a slow speed to let small stabilizing bubbles form, then increase the speed to high and beat until they form soft peaks. Gradually add the superfine sugar, a tablespoonful at a time, while beating on a high speed until all the sugar has dissolved into the egg whites. Test a little of the meringue mixture between your fingers, and if it feels gritty, keep beating until the mixture is smooth. Add the vanilla extract to the mixture and then slowly fold in the confectioners' sugar, using a spatula. The mixture should be glossy, at which point it is ready to pipe and bake. Once you have formed your meringue into the desired shapes, bake in a slow oven (225°F/110°C) until they have dried out, which will take at least an hour for smaller meringues and up to 3 hours for large pavlova nests.

TIPS

Use clean equipment when preparing the meringue mixture. Any trace of grease on mixing bowls or utensils will affect the consistency and volume of the meringue. Grease tends to cling to plastic, so if possible, mix your meringue in a glass or metal bowl.

Any trace of egg yolk will ruin your meringue. Resist the temptation to dip a finger into your bowl to get the yolk out. Some people use a piece of eggshell or a cotton-swab tip to remove the yolk, but it is often easiest just to discard that egg. For this reason, first separate your eggs into a small bowl and then add the egg whites individually to the larger mixing bowl. That way,

if some yolk slips through, you need only discard one egg white, not the whole batch.

If the sugar hasn't dissolved and the mixture is grainy when it goes into the oven, the meringues will often leak a sugar syrup during baking.

Baking the meringues at a low temperature allows for the gradual evaporation of the moisture from the meringue mixture. If the oven is too hot, the outside of the meringue will be crunchy and browned and the center will be chewy and sticky.

WHAT TO DO WITH ALL THE LEFTOVER EGG YOLKS?

There are plenty of recipes that call for just egg yolks, so don't throw away the yolks after you have made your meringue. Here's a simple vanilla custard recipe to get you started.

Vanilla Custard

1 vanilla bean
1¼ cups (300 ml) milk
4 extra-large egg yolks
½ cup (100 g) superfine sugar
generous ¼ cup (40 g) cornstarch

Split the vanilla bean with a knife and place it in a saucepan. Add the milk and bring to a boil, then remove the vanilla bean and turn off the heat. Meanwhile, using an electric mixer, beat the egg yolks, sugar, and cornstarch together until thick and glossy. Gradually add the warm milk while continuing to beat. Pour the mixture into a saucepan and stir it over medium heat until it boils and thickens. Cover the surface of the custard with plastic wrap and let cool.

Pomegranate-Honey Pavlovas

Pomegranate seeds have a naturally jewel-like look and a sweet-sour taste that marries really well with the sugary meringue of a pavlova. Honey and chopped pistachios in the topping all add up to an exotically Eastern palette of flavors. You can make the meringue bases a day or two ahead of time and store them in an airtight container, adding the filling and topping just before you serve.

1 Preheat the oven to 225°F/110°C. Line two baking sheets with parchment paper. Use a 1½-inch (4-cm) round cutter as a guide to trace 12 evenly spaced circles on each sheet of parchment paper in pencil. Turn the parchment paper over so that the pencil does not rub off on the meringues while they are baking.

2 Use a spatula to spread the meringue mixture inside each circle on the parchment paper. Each of these will form the base of a pavlova.

3 Spoon the remaining meringue mixture into a pastry bag fitted with a small round piping tip. Pipe a border of meringue around the edge of each base. Bake the pavlovas in the preheated oven for about 1 hour, or until they have dried out. Let the pavlovas cool completely on the baking sheets before adding the filling.

4 Meanwhile, blanch the pistachio nuts in boiling water for 10 minutes, then rub off their skins with a clean dish towel before finely crushing them. When ready to serve, stir the honey into the crème fraîche and then spoon some into each pavlova. Sprinkle with the crushed pistachio nuts and pomegranate seeds, then top with gold leaf to decorate, if desired.

To make 24

1 quantity of Meringue Mixture
(_see page 27_)
⅓ cup (50 g) shelled pistachio nuts
1 tsp honey
⅔ cup (150 g) crème fraîche
4 tbsp pomegranate seeds
edible gold leaf,
for decorating (optional)

ACTUAL SIZE

Micro-Meringue Kisses

Light as air and not much more calorific, only their delectable fillings hold these little sugar clouds down to earth. I've given you three different flavor options to fill them: Irish coffee cream, white chocolate and pistachio cream, and delicate rose Chantilly.

To make 40

½ quantity of Meringue Mixture (*see page 27*)

filling of your choice from the following options (each filling is enough to fill all the meringues)

IRISH COFFEE CREAM

1 tbsp instant coffee granules

1 tbsp superfine sugar

2 tsp boiling water

scant 1¼ cups (300 ml) heavy cream

2 tsp whiskey, or to taste

ROSE CHANTILLY

generous ¾ cup (175 ml) heavy cream

scant ¼ cup (25 g) confectioners' sugar, sifted

1 tsp rose water

pink food coloring (optional)

WHITE CHOCOLATE & PISTACHIO CREAM

scant ¼ cup (30 g) shelled pistachio nuts

2½ oz (70 g) white chocolate, broken into pieces

scant ⅔ cup (135 ml) heavy cream

1 tbsp confectioners' sugar

1 To make the Irish coffee cream filling, dissolve the coffee granules and sugar in the boiling water. Whip the cream in a bowl until it holds its shape, then stir in the coffee mixture and whiskey until well incorporated.

2 To make the rose Chantilly filling, whip the cream, sugar, and rose water in a bowl until thick. If desired, tint the mixture with pink food coloring.

3 To make the white chocolate and pistachio cream filling, blanch the pistachios in boiling water for 10 minutes, then rub off their skins with a clean dish towel before finely chopping them. Melt the chocolate (*see page 41*), then let it cool. Lightly whip the cream with the confectioners' sugar in a bowl, then stir in the melted chocolate and the chopped pistachio nuts.

4 Preheat the oven to 225°F/110°C. Line two baking sheets with parchment paper.

5 Spoon the meringue mixture into a pastry bag fitted with a small star piping tip. Pipe little rosettes about ¾ inch (2 cm) in diameter onto the lined baking sheets, then bake them in the preheated oven for about 1 hour, or until they have completely dried out. Let the meringues cool completely on the baking sheets before sandwiching them together with your chosen filling.

ACTUAL SIZE

Cinnamon Meringue Mushrooms

These adorable meringue mushrooms could easily be mistaken for the real thing. Don't worry about your piping skills—mushrooms grow in their own sweet way in nature and no two are alike; once the finished versions are assembled and decorated, they'll look so adorable that you won't notice the irregularities. Arrange a batch on a rustic wooden board to go with after-dinner coffee.

To make 50

1 tsp ground cinnamon

1 quantity of Meringue Mixture
(*see page 27*)

3½ oz (100 g) semisweet chocolate,
broken into pieces

unsweetened cocoa powder,
for dusting (optional)

1 Preheat the oven to 225°F/110°C. Line two baking sheets with parchment paper. Gently fold the cinnamon through the meringue mixture with a spatula. Spoon the meringue mixture into a pastry bag fitted with a small round piping tip. To make the tops of the mushrooms, pipe domed circles of meringue no more than 1 inch (2.5 cm) in diameter onto one of the lined baking sheets. On the second lined baking sheet, pipe a tapered stem for each mushroom by squeezing the piping bag to form a ½ inch (1 cm) round base and then slowly and evenly drawing the bag up to form a tapered stem about 1 inch (2.5 cm) tall.

2 Bake the meringues in the preheated oven for about 2 hours, or until they are completely dried out. Let them cool completely on the baking sheets.

3 To assemble the mushrooms, use a small knife to trim the pointy end of each stem. Melt the chocolate (*see page 41*), then use a small palette knife to spread it on the underside of each mushroom dome. Attach a stem to each dome by placing the trimmed end of the stem in the molten chocolate.

4 Place each mushroom, stem side up, on a tray until the chocolate has set. If desired, dust the tops of the mushrooms with cocoa powder. Store the meringue mushrooms in an airtight container for up to 3 weeks at room temperature.

ACTUAL SIZE

Mini Dacquoise Towers

With crunchy disks of almond and hazelnut meringue alternating with a gooey mocha mousse that is lightly set with gelatin, these minute dacquoises can really rock a cake stand for an "occasion" treat. They're best chilled in the refrigerator for half an hour or so, then lightly dusted with unsweetened cocoa powder just before serving.

1 To make the mocha mousse, first melt the chocolate (see page 41). In a small saucepan, bring the milk to a boil, then sprinkle the gelatin over it and whisk until combined. Pour the milk into the melted chocolate and stir in the coffee granules and coffee liqueur until smooth. Set the mixture aside to cool. Whip the cream in a bowl until soft peaks form, then fold it into the chocolate mixture. Spoon the mousse into a pastry bag fitted with a small petal tip and then refrigerate until required.

2 Preheat the oven to 350°F/180°C. Line a shallow 10-inch x 15-inch (25-cm x 38-cm) baking pan with parchment paper. Using an electric mixer, beat the egg whites until soft peaks form. Gradually add the confectioners' sugar while continuing to beat until the mixture is firm and glossy. Gently fold in the ground hazelnuts, ground almonds, and superfine sugar. Spread the batter evenly into the lined baking pan and bake in the preheated oven for about 15 minutes, or until firm to the touch. Use a 1-inch (2.5-cm) round cutter to cut out 30 circles from the meringue while it is still warm, then let cool completely on a wire rack before assembling.

3 To assemble the dacquoises, pipe a ruffle border of mousse onto 10 of the meringue circles, then place another circle on top of each one. Pipe another ruffled layer of mousse onto the second circle and then top with the remaining circles. If desired, dust with unsweetened cocoa before serving.

To make 10

6 extra-large egg whites
⅔ cup (75 g) confectioners' sugar, sifted
scant ½ cup (40 g) ground hazelnuts
generous ⅓ cup (35 g) ground almonds
scant ½ cup (85 g) superfine sugar
unsweetened cocoa powder, for dusting (optional)

MOCHA MOUSSE

5½ oz (150 g) semisweet chocolate, broken into pieces
4 tbsp milk
2 tsp powdered gelatin
2 tsp instant coffee granules
1 tbsp coffee liqueur
generous ¾ cup (200 ml) heavy cream

ACTUAL SIZE

Mini Violet & Green Tea Macarons

No petite treat lineup would be complete without macarons. These dainty examples are small enough to have earned the soubriquet "batchelor's buttons"—the everyday name for macarons when they were served at card parties in the nineteenth century. The violet and green tea flavors are subtle and unusual, and work wonderfully with a cup of smoky lapsang souchong tea.

To make 40

1 cup (125 g) confectioners' sugar

generous 1⅓ cups (125 g) ground almonds

3¼ oz (90 g) egg whites (3 large egg whites)

2 tbsp water

scant ½ cup (110 g) superfine sugar

purple and green food coloring

½ tsp violet extract/flavoring

⅔ cup (150 ml) heavy cream

1 tsp matcha green tea powder

1 Preheat the oven to 325°F/160°C. Line a large baking sheet with parchment paper. Place the confectioners' sugar, ground almonds, and half the egg whites in a large bowl and mix to a paste.

2 Put the water and superfine sugar into a small saucepan and gently stir over low heat until the sugar has dissolved. Increase the heat and let the mixture boil until it thickens to a syrup. Beat the remaining egg whites in a small bowl with a handheld electric mixer until medium-stiff peaks form, then add the sugar syrup, beating until the mixture becomes stiff and shiny. Stir in the almond paste. Divide the batter between two bowls. Tint one bowl with purple food coloring and the other bowl with green food coloring. Add the violet extract/flavoring to the purple batter.

3 Spoon the two batters into separate pastry bags, each fitted with a small round piping tip. Pipe flat ½-inch (1-cm) circles of meringue onto the lined baking sheet, about ¾ inch (2 cm) apart. Let the piped circles stand at room temperature for 30 minutes to form a skin, then bake in the preheated oven with the door slightly ajar for 8–10 minutes, until firm. Remove the macarons from the oven and let them cool completely on the baking sheet.

4 For the fillings, whip the cream until it holds its shape, then divide between two bowls. Stir the green tea powder into one bowl. Sandwich the purple macarons together with the plain whipped cream, and the green ones together with the green tea whipped cream.

ACTUAL SIZE

Chocolate

Chocolate

From its origins as a spicy drink enjoyed by Mayan Indians to its current status as a beloved confection, chocolate has always carried connotations of comfort and indulgence. The chocolate morsels in this chapter certainly punch well above their weight in sweet sophistication.

Ganache

Ganache is a mixture of melted chocolate and cream. It can be poured over bakes while still warm as a glaze, or cooled and beaten to achieve a spreadable consistency. Ganache can be stored in the refrigerator for about 2 weeks, or frozen for up to 3 months. Let the ganache stand at room temperature to soften before use.

---

7 oz (200 g) semisweet or milk chocolate or
12½ oz (360 g) white chocolate

½ cup (125 ml) heavy cream

---

1 Break the chocolate into small pieces and place it in a medium bowl.

2 Bring the cream to a boil in a small saucepan over medium heat.

3 Pour the hot cream over the chocolate and let it sit for 1–2 minutes before stirring it with a whisk until the mixture is smooth and all the chocolate has melted.

NOTE White chocolate can be a little difficult to work with, because it can split (become grainy) if it is overheated. Adding more white chocolate (as compared to milk or semisweet chocolate) in proportion to the amount of cream will help to overcome this problem.

CHOOSING CHOCOLATE FOR BAKING

There is a huge range of eating and cooking chocolate—the difference between all the brands depends on the type of cocoa beans used, the proportion of cocoa solids and cocoa butter, the sugar content, and flavorings. When buying chocolate, it is important to read the list of ingredients. Look at the percentage of cocoa solids and sugar, because this indicates the taste of the chocolate. The higher the cocoa content, the more "chocolaty" it will be.

Semisweet chocolate with a minimum of 70 percent cocoa solids is best for most baking recipes. You should use a chocolate that you would enjoy eating on its own.

MELTING CHOCOLATE

You don't need a double boiler (or bain-marie) to melt chocolate—you can make a double boiler by setting a heatproof bowl over a saucepan of simmering water. Make sure the bottom of the bowl doesn't touch the water in the saucepan. Place the chocolate, broken into pieces, in the bowl and stir until it has melted. The chocolate will be heated by the steam trapped in the saucepan. When you have finished, remove the bowl from the pan and dry the bottom before tipping the chocolate out, to make sure that water doesn't spill into the chocolate and ruin it.

Alternatively, you can melt chocolate in a microwave, preferably on a low (50 percent) power setting, to avoid scorching it. Place the chocolate in a microwave-safe bowl and heat in short bursts of 30 seconds, stirring in between. How long it will take the chocolate to melt will depend on the wattage of the microwave, quantity of chocolate, and even the cocoa butter content. Finish heating when most, but not all, of the chocolate is melted. Remove from the microwave and stir the chocolate constantly until it is smooth and completely melted.

MAKING CHOCOLATE DECORATIONS

Chocolate decorations can be easily made using silicone or plastic molds. Simply pour melted chocolate into the molds, tap them against the counter to remove any air bubbles, and then place them in the freezer. After about 10 minutes, the chocolate will be set and should easily pop out when the molds are flexed.

Gilded Caramel Shortbread Squares

Tiny squares of caramel- and chocolate-topped shortbread are given a precious finish with a light dusting of edible gold luster dust. Arrange them in a pyramid on the serving plate and they'll look like a little stack of gold bullion—but with the bonus that they taste delicious. If you're short of time, you can replace the cooked caramel with a layer of dulce de leche (caramel sauce), which you can find in jars in most supermarkets.

To make about 115

1¾ cups (250 g) all-purpose flour
generous ⅓ cup (75 g) superfine sugar
1½ sticks (175 g) unsalted butter, softened and cubed, plus extra for greasing

CARAMEL LAYER

7 tbsp (100 g) unsalted butter
½ cup (100 g) firmly packed dark brown sugar
two 14-oz (397-g) cans condensed milk

TOPPING

7 oz (200 g) milk chocolate, broken into pieces
edible gold luster dust, for decorating

1 Preheat the oven to 350°F/180°C. Lightly grease a 13-inch x 9-inch (33-cm x 23-cm) jellyroll pan. To make the shortbread, mix the flour and sugar together in a bowl. Rub in the butter with your fingertips until the mixture resembles fine bread crumbs. Knead the mixture together until it forms a dough, then press it evenly into the bottom of the prepared pan. Prick the shortbread lightly with a fork and bake in the preheated oven for about 20 minutes, or until firm to the touch and very lightly browned. Let the shortbread cool completely in the pan.

2 To make the caramel layer, place the butter, sugar, and condensed milk in a small saucepan and gently heat until the sugar has dissolved. Bring the mixture to a boil while stirring constantly, then reduce the heat and simmer gently, stirring, for about 5 minutes, or until the mixture has thickened slightly. Pour the caramel over the shortbread and let it cool to room temperature.

3 For the topping, melt the chocolate (*see page 41*), then pour it over the cold caramel and let it set before cutting the shortbread into 1-inch (2.5-cm) squares. Use a soft paintbrush to dust the top of each square with edible gold luster dust before serving.

ACTUAL SIZE

Chocolate Brownies with Salted Caramel Frosting

Chocolate and salted caramel is one of the classic flavor combinations, and these delectable little brownie flowers deliver a lot of taste for their delicate size. Your cooked brownie should have cooled completely before you cut out the shapes. If it's still a little warm, you'll find it hard to get clean edges on your flowers.

1 Preheat the oven to 350°F/180°C. Line the bottom of a shallow 8-inch (20-cm) square baking pan with parchment paper. To make the brownies, place the butter cubes and chocolate pieces in a heatproof bowl set over a small saucepan of simmering water until both have melted, stirring occasionally until mixed and smooth. Remove from the pan and let cool to room temperature.

2 In a separate bowl, use an electric mixer to beat the eggs and sugar together on high speed for about 5 minutes, until the mixture is thick and creamy and has doubled in volume. Pour the cooled chocolate mixture over the egg-and-sugar mixture, then gently fold all the ingredients together with a spatula. Sift in the flour and cocoa powder and gently combine until the mixture is a sticky, fudgelike consistency. Pour the batter into the prepared baking pan and spread it into the corners with a spatula. Bake in the preheated oven for about 25 minutes, or until the top is shiny and the sides are just beginning to come away from the pan. Let the brownie cool completely in the pan.

3 To make the frosting, use an electric mixer to beat the butter and sugar together in a bowl for at least 5 minutes, then gradually add the dulce de leche, vanilla extract, and salt while continuing to beat. Place in a pastry bag fitted with a small star tip.

4 To assemble the brownies, use a small flower-shape cutter (or another shape of your choice) to cut out 24 flower-shape brownie bites. Pipe a zigzag of frosting on top of each brownie, then decorate each with a gold sugar flower, if desired.

To make 24

1½ sticks (175 g) unsalted butter, cubed

6½ oz (185 g) dark chocolate, broken into pieces

3 extra-large eggs

generous 1⅓ cups (275 g) superfine sugar

scant ⅔ cup (85 g) all-purpose flour

scant ½ cup (40 g) unsweetened cocoa powder

gold sugar flowers, for decorating (optional)

SALTED CARAMEL FROSTING

1½ sticks (175 g) salted butter, softened

1¾ cups (200 g) confectioners' sugar, sifted

3 tbsp dulce de leche (caramel sauce)

1 tsp vanilla extract

½ tsp salt

ACTUAL SIZE

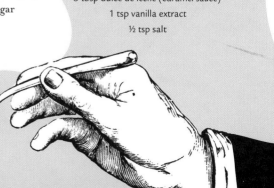

Chocolate Cups with Mango Mousse

Crisp chocolate shells filled with a light and tangy mousse, these tiny delights are part candy, part dessert. The lime juice gives the mousse a slight citrus kick, keeping the finished treat from tasting too sweet. Use the darkest chocolate you can find to make the shells—70 percent cocoa solids or higher will result in the perfect trio of bitter chocolate, sharp lime, and cool, fruity mango.

To make 12

5½ oz (150 g) semisweet chocolate, broken into pieces

heaping 1 tsp powdered gelatin

2 tbsp cold water

½ mango, peeled, pitted, and pureed

1 tbsp fresh lime juice

½ cup (60 g) confectioners' sugar

½ cup (125 g) plain yogurt

generous 1 cup (250 ml) heavy cream, whipped until it holds its shape

fresh mint sprigs, for decorating (optional)

1 To make the chocolate cups, melt the chocolate (*see page 41*), then use a small paintbrush to paint half the melted chocolate evenly on the inside of 12 mini paper liners or silicone cupcake cups. Place the liners or cups on a baking sheet and put them in the freezer until set. Use the remaining melted chocolate to paint on a second layer and then freeze again until firm. Remove from the freezer and carefully peel away the liners or cups to reveal the chocolate cups.

2 To make the mango mousse, soak the gelatin in the cold water in a bowl. Mix the mango puree, lime juice, and confectioners' sugar together in a saucepan over low heat and bring to a light boil. Stir in the gelatin mixture and then remove the pan from the heat and pour the contents into a bowl. Let the mixture cool by placing the bowl on top of a bowl filled with ice. While the mixture is cooling, vigorously beat it while gradually adding the yogurt. Gently fold in the whipped cream to finish.

3 Place the mango mousse in a pastry bag fitted with a small star piping tip and pipe a star of mango mousse into each chocolate cup. Decorate each with a mint sprig, if desired.

ACTUAL SIZE

Pistachio & White Chocolate Florentines

Sweet, sticky, and crunchy all at once, Florentines make the perfect afternoon treat. These miniature versions stand out flavorwise with an unusual combination of cranberries and pistachios instead of the customary cherries and almonds or hazelnuts. If you keep the proportions the same, you can experiment with your own fruit-and-nut combinations to put your stamp on the recipe.

1 Preheat the oven to 350°F/180°C. Line the bottom of a 9-inch x 13-inch (23-cm x 33-cm) baking sheet with parchment paper. Melt the butter together with the sugar in a saucepan over low heat. Use a spoon to beat in the flour, cream, and lemon juice. Chop the pistachio nuts and dried cranberries, then stir them into the mixture with the slivered almonds.

2 Spread the Florentine mixture evenly onto the lined baking sheet and then bake in the preheated oven for about 15 minutes until golden but not brown. Remove the baking sheet from the oven and quickly use a 1-inch (2.5-cm) round cutter to cut out 30 circles from the Florentine bake while it is still hot. Let the circles cool completely on a clean, lined baking sheet.

3 Melt the chocolate (*see page 41*), then dip the backs of the cooled Florentines in the melted chocolate to coat and place, chocolate side down, on the lined baking sheet. Transfer the baking sheet to the refrigerator for about 20 minutes, until the chocolate has set. Drizzle the remaining melted chocolate over the tops of the Florentines and return to the refrigerator for an additional 10 minutes, until set, before serving.

TIP You can also bake the Florentine mixture in the sections of silicone mini muffin baking pans.

To make 30

3 tbsp (40 g) unsalted butter

¼ cup (50 g) superfine sugar

1 tbsp all-purpose flour

1 tbsp heavy cream

1 tsp fresh lemon juice

⅓ cup (50 g) shelled pistachio nuts, skins removed (*see page 29*)

¼ cup (40 g) dried cranberries

½ cup (50 g) slivered almonds

3½ oz (100 g) white chocolate, broken into pieces

ACTUAL SIZE

Pastry

Pastry

There are many different types of pastry, but if you only want to turn to one kind, then probably the most useful and versatile pastry is flaky pastry dough, which has both a sweet and savory version, making it ideal for creating a whole range of mini bites to suit different tastes.

Flaky Pastry Dough (pâte brisée)

Flaky pastry dough is made using a "half-fat-to-flour" ratio. Fat (such as butter) is rubbed into all-purpose flour to create a loose mixture that is bound together with iced water. If you don't want to get your fingers dirty, it can also be made with a pastry blender or food processor. For both methods, once the dough is made, wrap it in plastic wrap and chill in the refrigerator for 10–15 minutes before using.

scant 1 cup (125 g) all-purpose flour
pinch of salt
4 tbsp (55 g) unsalted butter, cubed
2–3 tbsp iced water

METHOD 1 (BY HAND)

Place the flour and salt in a large bowl and add the cubes of butter.

Use your fingertips to rub the butter into the flour until the mixture resembles coarse bread crumbs with no large lumps of butter remaining. Lift the mixture up as you rub the butter in so that the air going through it keeps it cool. Shake the bowl intermittently to bring the lumps of butter to the surface. Work quickly so that the mixture does not become greasy.

Stir in just enough of the iced water to bind the dough together.

METHOD 2 (FOOD PROCESSOR)

Alternatively, put the flour, salt, and butter in a food processor and pulse until the fat is rubbed into the flour. With the motor running, gradually add the iced water through the feed tube until the dough comes together. Add just enough water to bind it and then stop.

Sweet Flaky Pastry Dough (pâte sucrée)

This rich, sweet pastry makes a delicious crust for tarts or fruit pies.

7 tbsp (100 g) unsalted butter, softened
⅓ cup (60 g) superfine sugar
3 extra-large egg yolks
scant 1½ cups (200 g) all-purpose flour, plus extra for dusting

Beat the butter and sugar together in a bowl until light and fluffy, then beat in the egg yolks one at a time, until completely incorporated.

Mix in the flour until the mixture comes together as a ball of dough. Turn the dough out onto a floured counter and knead until smooth.

Wrap the dough in plastic wrap and chill in the refrigerator for at least an hour. Alternatively, it can be frozen for use at a later date.

FREEZING PASTRY DOUGH

Wrap the dough tightly in plastic wrap, place in a freezer-safe bag, and freeze for up to 2 months. Thaw the dough in the refrigerator for 3–4 hours before rolling and shaping. Fully baked unfilled pastry shells can be stored in an airtight container at room temperature for up to 3 days.

BAKING PASTRY DOUGH

Common practice with tartlets is to line and fill the pastry shells with pie weights, dried beans, or rice before baking to prevent the dough from shrinking and puffing up. You can eliminate this step by putting the unbaked pastry shells in the freezer for 15 minutes to set the dough and prevent it from shrinking during baking. You can also prick the bottom of the pastry shells with a fork before baking to help maintain their shape.

Mini Mille-Feuilles with Elderflower Cream

Confected from the lightest puff pastry (in French, *millefeuille* means "thousand leaves"), thin slices of strawberry and cream infused with the understated but heady flavor of elderflower, these diminutive pastries look elegant and taste like the essence of a sunny summer's day.

To make 24

13 oz (375 g) ready-to-bake puff pastry, just thawed if frozen

1 tbsp elderflower syrup

2 tsp superfine sugar

½ cup (125 ml) heavy cream

10 fresh strawberries, hulled and thinly sliced

confectioners' sugar, for dusting

1 Preheat the oven to 400°F/200°C. Line a large baking sheet with parchment paper. Cut the puff pastry sheet into small rectangles 2 inches (5 cm) long and 1 inch (2.5 cm) wide. Arrange on the lined baking sheet and use a fork to prick holes into the surface of each one. Place a sheet of parchment paper over the top of the pastries.

2 Place another baking sheet on top of the pastries (to stop the pastry from rising too much during baking), then bake in the preheated oven for 10–15 minutes, until golden. Let the puff pastry layers cool completely on the baking sheet.

3 Mix the elderflower syrup and superfine sugar into the cream in a bowl and then beat until thick. To assemble each mille-feuille, spread the cream over a pastry layer, then top with strawberries and another layer of pastry. Spread more cream on top of the second pastry layer, then top with strawberries and a final pastry layer. Dust the top of each mille-feuille with confectioners' sugar before serving.

TIP The puff pastry layers can be baked ahead of time and stored in an airtight container.

ACTUAL SIZE

Heart-Shape Vol-au-Vents with Raspberry Coulis

Literally French for "windblown," conveying just how light they are, these vol-au-vents are more usually found with savory fillings—but this sweet, nutty, chocolaty version is full of flavor, and the heart shape adds an extra cute touch. A drizzle of raspberry coulis added just before serving will make them look as delicious as they taste.

1 To make the raspberry coulis, place the raspberries, sugar, and lemon juice in a saucepan and heat until the raspberries start to break down. Transfer the mixture to a food processor and blend until smooth. Pass through a fine strainer to remove the seeds, then set aside until ready to serve.

2 Preheat the oven to 350°F/180°C. Line two or three baking sheets with parchment paper. Lay the puff pastry sheet on a floured counter and use a small heart cutter, no more than 1½ inches (4 cm) at its widest point, to cut out 80 heart shapes. Use a slightly smaller heart cutter to cut a small heart out of the center of half the quantity of hearts—these will be the heart rings. Use a fork to prick holes in the plain hearts. Brush egg wash around the edge of the plain hearts, then place the heart rings on top of the plain hearts. Be careful to make sure that the egg wash does not drip down the sides, otherwise the pastry will not rise. Place the hearts on the lined baking sheets, then place them in the freezer for 5 minutes, or until firm.

3 Brush the tops of the hearts with egg wash before baking them in the preheated oven for 12 minutes, or until golden brown. Let them cool completely on the baking sheets.

4 Use a spoon to gently remove the center of each vol-au-vent, then fill with the chocolate ganache. If desired, decorate with the finely chopped roasted hazelnuts and a light dusting of cocoa powder, then serve with a drizzle of the raspberry coulis.

TIP Reserve the puff pastry scraps for using in other recipes, such as the palmiers on page 58 or the cheese straws on page 124.

To make 40

13 oz (375 g) ready-to-bake
puff pastry, just thawed if frozen

all-purpose flour, for dusting

egg wash (1 extra-large egg
beaten with 1 tbsp cold water)

1 quantity of Dark
Chocolate Ganache
(*see page 41*)

⅓ cup (50 g) roasted blanched
hazelnuts, finely chopped,
for decorating (optional)

unsweetened cocoa powder,
for dusting (optional)

RASPBERRY COULIS

2 cups (250 g) raspberries,
fresh or frozen

1 tbsp confectioners'
sugar

juice of ½ lemon

ACTUAL SIZE

Chai-Spiced Palmiers

Indian-inspired chai spicing is becoming more popular in cappuccinos and lattes, but it's still uncommon as a flavoring for cakes or cookies. However, the delicious chai mixture of cinnamon, ginger, cardamom, and cloves is presented here as a filling for the tasty, crisp pastries known colloquially as elephant's ears. Kitten's ears, perhaps, in this miniature form?

To make 50

generous ½ cup (115 g) superfine sugar, plus extra (optional) for sprinkling

1½ tsp ground cinnamon

½ tsp ground ginger

½ tsp ground cloves

½ tsp ground cardamom

6½ oz (190 g) ready-to-bake puff pastry, just thawed if frozen

2½ tbsp (30 g) butter, melted and cooled

1 Mix the sugar with the cinnamon, ginger, cloves, and cardamom in a bowl. Unwrap the puff pastry and lay it on a clean counter. Sprinkle the chai sugar mixture over the pastry then roll a nonstick rolling pin over the top of the pastry to help the chai sugar stick to it.

2 Cut the pastry into strips 3 inches (7.5 cm) wide. Tightly roll both sides of each pastry strip inward so that they meet in the middle. Wrap the rolled logs in plastic wrap and chill in the refrigerator for about 30 minutes, or until firm. Meanwhile, preheat the oven to 400°F/200°C. Line two baking sheets with parchment paper.

3 Slice the firm pastry logs into thin slices with a serrated knife and place the slices, evenly spaced and cut side up, on the lined baking sheets. Brush each palmier with melted butter and sprinkle with extra sugar, if desired. Bake in the preheated oven for 5 minutes, or until caramelized and brown, then turn over with a spatula and bake for an additional 3–5 minutes, until caramelized on the other side. Transfer to a wire rack to cool.

TIP This is a great recipe for using up leftover scraps of puff pastry.

ACTUAL SIZE

Baked Raspberry Tartlets

Crisp, sweet paté sucrée is used to make these tartlet shells, which are then finished with a brown butter filling and topped off with a fresh raspberry. Brown butter lends the tartlets a tasty, slightly "nutty" flavor; having used it once, you'll probably find plenty of other applications for it when you bake.

To make 36

1 quantity of Sweet Flaky Pastry Dough (*see page 53*)

confectioners' sugar, for dusting

BROWN BUTTER FILLING

1 stick (115 g) unsalted butter, plus extra for greasing

½ cup (100 g) superfine sugar

2 extra-large eggs

1 tsp vanilla extract

pinch of salt

¼ cup (35 g) all-purpose flour, plus extra for dusting

scant ⅔ cup (75 g) raspberries, fresh or frozen

1 Grease individual mini tartlet pans—those used here measured 1½ inches (4 cm) in length (you can prepare and bake the tartlets in batches according to how many pans you may have). Roll out the dough on a lightly floured counter to about ¼ inch (5 mm) thick. If using almond-shape mini tartlet pans like those here, use a rectangular cutter to cut out rectangles of dough that are wider and longer than the pans. Drape the dough into the prepared tartlet pans, gently pushing the dough into the bottom edges and against the pan sides to make strong pastry shells. Press down firmly along the rims of the pans to cut off the excess dough. Use a fork to prick holes all over the bottoms and sides of the tartlet shells. Place on a baking sheet, then place in the freezer for at least 30 minutes, until firm. Meanwhile, preheat the oven to 350°F/180°C.

2 Bake the tartlet shells in the preheated oven for 7–8 minutes, until they are lightly golden.

3 To make the filling, melt the butter in a small saucepan over low heat, then increase the heat to medium and cook it until there are brown flecks on the bottom of the pan. The butter will foam up and then settle back down again while browning and will produce a nutty aroma. Remove from the heat.

4 Beat the sugar, eggs, vanilla extract, and salt together in a bowl with a whisk. Whisk in the flour gently, then pour in the browned butter in a steady stream while whisking constantly. Place a raspberry in each tartlet shell, then pour the filling over them until almost filling the shell. Return to the oven for 10 minutes, until golden brown and the filling is set. Let the tartlets cool completely in the pans before removing and serving with a dusting of confectioners' sugar.

ACTUAL SIZE

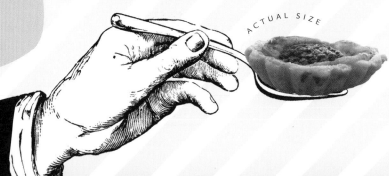

Lemon-Lime Gems

The combination of crisp, sweet flaky pastry dough and sharp homemade lemon and lime curd ensure these morsels are gobbled up quickly whatever the occasion. The tartlet shells can be baked ahead of time and frozen—if you have a jar of lemon-lime curd on hand, you'll never be more than 20 minutes away from a batch of zingy gems.

1 To make the lemon-lime curd, whisk the lemon juice, lime juice, sugar, and eggs together in a medium heatproof bowl. Add the butter, then set the bowl over a small saucepan of simmering water. Cook the curd, while stirring often, for at least 8 minutes, or until it thickens and coats the back of a spoon. Remove from the pan, let cool, stirring occasionally, then cover with plastic wrap and store the curd in the refrigerator until required.

2 Grease individual mini tartlet pans—those used here measured 1 inch (2.5 cm) in diameter (you can prepare and bake the tartlets in batches according to how many pans you may have). Roll out the dough on a lightly floured counter to about ¼ inch (5 mm) thick. Use a 2-inch (5-cm) round cutter to cut out circles of dough. Drape the dough circles into the prepared tartlet pans, gently pushing the dough into the bottom edges and against the pan sides to make strong pastry shells. Press down firmly along the rims of the pans to cut off the excess dough. Use a fork to prick holes all over the bottoms and sides of the tartlet shells. Place on a baking sheet, then place in the freezer for at least 30 minutes, until firm. Meanwhile, preheat the oven to 350°F/180°C.

3 Bake the tartlet shells in the preheated oven for 7–8 minutes, until golden brown. Let cool completely in the pans, then remove and divide the lemon-lime curd among them.

To make 48

1 quantity of Sweet Flaky Pastry Dough
(*see page 53*)

all-purpose flour, for dusting

LEMON-LIME CURD

4 tbsp fresh lemon juice

4 tbsp fresh lime juice

¼ cup (55 g) superfine sugar

4 extra-large eggs,
at room temperature

7 tbsp (100 g) unsalted butter,
chopped

ACTUAL SIZE

Chocolate Ganache-Filled Tartlets

Rich chocolate dough is baked in tiny fluted tartlet pans, then filled with a creamy white chocolate ganache and decorated with melted chocolate. You can prebake the shells several hours ahead, but don't store them in the refrigerator, or the dough will lose its crispness.

To make 24

generous ½ cup (85 g)
all-purpose flour,
plus extra for dusting

2 tbsp unsweetened cocoa powder

4½ tbsp (60 g) unsalted butter,
softened and cubed,
plus extra for greasing

2 tbsp superfine sugar

1 extra-large egg yolk

FILLING & DECORATION

1 quantity of warm White
Chocolate Ganache
(*see page 41*)

3½ oz (100 g) milk chocolate,
melted (*see page 41*; optional)

1 To make the dough, sift the flour and cocoa powder into a large mixing bowl, then rub in the butter with your fingertips until the mixture resembles fine bread crumbs. Mix in the sugar and egg yolk to form a soft dough. If the mixture is too dry, add a little cold water. Wrap the dough in plastic wrap and chill it in the refrigerator for an hour.

2 Preheat the oven to 350°F/180°C. Grease individual mini tartlet pans—those used here measured 1½ inches (4 cm) square (you can prepare and bake the tartlets in batches according to how many pans you may have). Roll out the dough on a lightly floured counter to about ¼ inch (5 mm) thick. Use a small knife to cut out 24 squares slightly larger than your mini tartlet pans. Drape the dough squares into the prepared pans, gently pushing the dough into the bottom edges and against the pan sides to make strong pastry shells. Press down firmly along the rims of the pans to cut off the excess dough. Use a fork to prick holes all over the bottoms and sides of the tartlet shells. Place on a baking sheet, then place in the freezer for at least 30 minutes, until firm.

3 Bake the tartlet shells in the preheated oven for 8–10 minutes, until crisp. Let cool in the pans, then remove and fill each one with the white chocolate ganache. Let them set at room temperature for several hours. If desired, fill a small pastry bag fitted with a small round piping tip with the melted milk chocolate and pipe drops on the tartlets to decorate. Let set before serving.

ACTUAL SIZE

Choux

Choux

Choux pastry is a light, twice-cooked pastry made with all-purpose flour, butter, water, and eggs. It is most commonly used to make profiteroles, éclairs, and choux puffs—here scaled down to diminutive form—but it serves equally well for savory pastries.

Choux Pastry (pâte à choux)

4 tbsp (55 g) unsalted butter
generous ¾ cup (180 ml) water
¾ cup (105 g) all-purpose flour
3 extra-large eggs, lightly beaten

Combine the butter with the water in a medium saucepan and bring the mixture to a boil. Add the flour, all at once, and beat with a wooden spoon over medium heat until the mixture forms a smooth ball. Transfer the mixture to a small bowl and beat in the eggs, one at a time, with a handheld electric mixer until the mixture becomes smooth and glossy. The choux pastry is now ready to pipe and bake.

Note: When making choux pastry, it is important to be sure that each egg is fully incorporated into the batter before adding the next. Don't worry if the batter separates and looks curdled at first. Keep beating, and it will come together.

BAKING CHOUX PASTRY

Choux pastry needs a hot oven, so it is important to preheat the oven and make sure it has come up to temperature before baking the choux pastries.

Bake the choux pastries one sheet at a time. Choux pastry rises when the water held in the pastry turns to steam in the heat of the oven, so too many sheets in the oven at one time will create too much humidity and your choux pastries won't be able to dry out and will be soggy and collapse. The additional batches can wait for their turn in the oven without any problems.

Resist the temptation to peek inside the oven during the baking time. Opening the door will release heat from the oven, which will affect how much the pastries puff up. Choux pastries are golden brown when they are completely baked.

Choux pastries are generally slit with a knife during or after baking to let steam escape from the inside. After releasing the steam, return the pastries to the oven for a few minutes to dry out before filling.

Choux pastry tastes best on the day it is made, but this is not always practical. Instead, the pastry can be made the day before, left in a covered bowl, and refrigerated overnight. You can then pipe and bake the pastry the following day. Alternatively, unfilled cooked choux pastries, such as éclairs and cream puffs, can be frozen in plastic containers. When you are ready to use them, thaw the frozen pastries on baking sheets and put them into a hot oven for 5 minutes, or let them stand in their containers to thaw at room temperature for an hour or so.

FILLING CHOUX PASTRY

Most fillings will start to soften the pastry once they have been piped inside. Choux pastries should, therefore, ideally be eaten within a couple of hours of filling.

SAVORY TREATS

Crisp choux pastry is versatile and delicious in savory recipes. To boost the flavor when making savory dishes, add a little salt and black pepper or some grated cheese or spices to the choux pastry dough before baking it.

Cute Croquembouches

The classic *croquembouche*—literally "something that crunches in the mouth"—is a tower of crisp choux puffs, filled with crème patissière and drizzled with toffee, which is often served at a wedding or first communion. These minute versions, stuck together with vanilla custard and spun toffee, take a little time to put together, but would add a festive touch to a special party—and they're tiny, so no need to share!

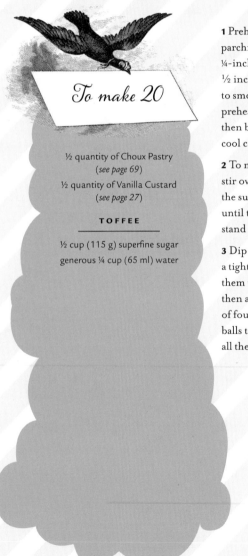

To make 20

½ quantity of Choux Pastry
(*see page 69*)
½ quantity of Vanilla Custard
(*see page 27*)

TOFFEE

½ cup (115 g) superfine sugar
generous ¼ cup (65 ml) water

1 Preheat the oven to 425°F/220°C. Line two to three baking sheets with parchment paper. Spoon the choux pastry into a pastry bag fitted with a ¼-inch (5-mm) round piping tip. Pipe 320 small balls of pastry about ½ inch (1 cm) apart onto the lined baking sheets. Use a damp pastry brush to smooth the top of each ball if they have peaks before baking them in the preheated oven for 7 minutes. Reduce the oven temperature to 350°F/180°C, then bake for an additional 5 minutes, or until the choux balls are crisp. Let cool completely on the baking sheets.

2 To make the toffee, combine the sugar and water in a small saucepan and stir over medium heat without boiling until the sugar has dissolved. Bring the sugar mixture to a boil and let it simmer, uncovered and without stirring, until the mixture is golden. Remove the pan from the heat and let the toffee stand for a few minutes until any bubbles subside.

3 Dip one side of seven choux balls into the custard, then arrange them in a tight circle about 1½ inches (4 cm) in diameter; the custard will help stick them together. Dip the bottom of another five choux balls into the custard, then arrange them in a circle on top of the other choux balls. Dip the bottom of four more choux balls into the custard, then arrange on top of the choux balls to complete the cone shape. Spin the toffee around the cone to secure all the choux balls in place. Make up the other *croquembouches* in the same way.

ACTUAL SIZE

Feathered Chocolate Éclairs

Éclairs were originally named *pain à la duchesse* **and these versions, miniaturized and with neatly feathered glazed tops, are certainly treats fit for any modern lady of fashion. Choux is one of the more forgiving pastries to cook with, provided that you remember to cut the puffs to release the steam inside as soon as you take them out of the oven.**

To make 50

1 quantity of Choux Pastry
(*see page 69*)
1¼ cups (300 ml) heavy cream
½ tsp vanilla extract

CHOCOLATE GLAZE

2 tbsp (25 g) unsalted butter,
cubed
3½ oz (100 g) semisweet
chocolate, broken into pieces
generous ¾ cup (90 g)
confectioners' sugar, sifted
scant ½ cup (100 ml) boiling water

WHITE ICING (OPTIONAL,
FOR FEATHERED ICING
PATTERN)

1 tbsp confectioners' sugar,
mixed with 1 drop of water

1 Preheat the oven to 400°F/200°C. Line two or three baking sheets with parchment paper. Spoon the choux pastry into a pastry bag fitted with a ¼-inch (5-mm) round piping tip. Pipe 50 small, thin lines of choux pastry about 1½ inches (4 cm) long, evenly spaced apart, onto the lined baking sheets. Use a damp pastry brush to smooth the top of each line of choux pastry before baking them in the preheated oven for 10 minutes. Cut a small horizontal slit at the end of each éclair to let the steam escape, then return them to the oven for an additional 5 minutes. Let cool completely on a wire rack.

2 Whip the cream in a bowl until it holds its shape, then stir in the vanilla extract. Fill a pastry bag fitted with a small round piping tip with the cream. Insert the tip into the slit in each éclair and gently squeeze the pastry bag so that the cream fills the cavity. A little cream will come back out of the slit if the éclair is completely filled.

3 To make the chocolate glaze, stir the butter, chocolate, and sugar together in a heatproof bowl set over a small saucepan of simmering water until the mixture is glossy and smooth. Gradually stir in the boiling water until the mixture loosens and reaches the consistency of thick cream. Use a small spatula to spread the glaze over the top of each éclair. If desired, pipe thin lines of white icing into the wet chocolate glaze across the width of the éclair, and drag a toothpick from one end of the éclair to the other to create a feathered pattern.

ACTUAL SIZE

Rose Religieuses

Practice your piping skills before undertaking a batch of these flowery little religieuses, so called because the original chocolate-glazed, cream-piped versions were thought to look like nuns in black-and-white habits. They're not hard to make, but you need to be neat. I opted for a dazzling fuchsia glaze on my rose-flavored minis, but if you prefer a more subtle effect you could pick a paler pink.

1 Preheat the oven to 400°F/200°C. Line two or three baking sheets with parchment paper. Spoon the choux pastry into a pastry bag fitted with a ¼-inch (5-mm) round piping tip. Pipe 24 balls about 1 inch (2.5 cm) in diameter and 24 smaller balls about ½ inch (1 cm) in diameter onto the lined baking sheets. Bake in the preheated oven for 10–12 minutes. Cut a small horizontal slit in the bottom of each ball to let the steam escape, then return them to the oven for 5 minutes. Let cool completely on a wire rack.

2 To make the crème patissière, bring the milk and vanilla extract to a boil in a small saucepan, then simmer for a few minutes. Let the mixture cool. Beat the egg yolks and sugar together in a large bowl with a handheld electric mixer or whisk until they are pale, then beat in the flour and cornstarch. Pour the milk into the mixture while beating constantly. Transfer the mixture to the saucepan and then gently bring it to a boil while beating constantly. Turn off the heat, then pour the mixture into a clean bowl, cover with plastic wrap, and let cool. Chill for several hours or overnight before use.

3 To make the rose icing, add the rose water and fuchsia food coloring to the sugar in a bowl and mix with a spoon until smooth. The icing should be thick and have the consistency of thick cream. If it is too runny, stir in more sugar, 1 teaspoon at a time, until the desired consistency is achieved

4 To fill the choux buns, place the crème patissière in a pastry bag fitted with a small round piping tip. Insert the tube into the slit in each choux bun and gently squeeze the pastry bag so that the crème patissière fills the cavity. A little crème patissière will come back out of the slit if the choux bun is completely filled.

5 Spread the icing on the top of the choux buns, using a small spatula, and then stick the small choux buns on top of the larger ones while the icing is still wet. If desired, place a small edible pearl or silver ball on top of each religieuse.

6 Fit a pastry bag with a small star piping tip and fill with the buttercream. Pipe lines of buttercream up from the bottom of the top choux bun to the icing. Refrigerate until ready to serve. The religieuses will keep in the refrigerator for up to 2 days.

To make 24

1 quantity of Choux Pastry
(*see page 69*)
⅓ quantity of Vanilla Buttercream
(*see page 13*)
small edible pearls or silver balls,
for decorating (optional)

CRÈME PATISSIÈRE

1 cup (225 ml) milk
1 tsp vanilla extract
3 extra-large egg yolks
½ cup (100 g) superfine sugar
2 tbsp all-purpose flour
2 tbsp cornstarch

ROSE ICING

½ tsp rose water
fuchsia pink food coloring
scant 1⅔ cups (200 g)
confectioners' sugar

ACTUAL SIZE

Caramel-Amaretto Paris-Brest Miniatures

Invented in 1891 to commemorate the Paris-Brest cycle race, the classic recipe for these choux rings usually flavors them with coffee. The petits fours-scaled pastries shown here have an almondy amaretto-crème filling instead and a sticky caramel glaze on top. Small sugar pearls add some shimmer to the end result.

To make 30

1 quantity of Choux Pastry
(*see page* 69)
edible pearls, for decorating
(optional)

AMARETTO CRÈME FILLING

⅔ cup (150 ml) heavy cream
1 tbsp amaretto, or to taste

CARAMEL GLAZE

3½ tbsp (50 g) unsalted butter
⅓ cup (60 g) firmly packed dark
brown sugar
2 tbsp glucose syrup
2 tbsp milk
1 cup (125 g) confectioners' sugar,
sifted

1 Preheat the oven to 400°F/200°C. Line two or three baking sheets with parchment paper. Spoon the choux pastry into a pastry bag fitted with a ¼-inch (5-mm) round piping tip. Pipe 30 rings about 1½ inches (4 cm) in diameter, evenly spaced apart, onto the lined baking sheets. Use a damp pastry brush to smooth the top of each ring before baking them in the preheated oven for 10 minutes. Cut a small horizontal slit in each ring to let the steam escape, then return them to the oven for an additional 5 minutes. Slice each ring horizontally in half and then let cool completely on a wire rack.

2 To make the amaretto crème filling, whip the cream to stiff peaks in a bowl with a handheld electric mixer, then gently stir in the amaretto with a spoon. Place the cream in a pastry bag fitted with a small star piping tip and pipe small dabs of cream between the ring halves.

3 To make the caramel glaze, heat the butter, brown sugar, and glucose syrup in a small saucepan over medium heat, stirring, until the butter and sugar have melted and the mixture begins to boil. Whisk in the milk, and then add the confectioners' sugar. Continue to whisk the mixture until it is smooth and thickened. Remove the caramel from the heat and let it cool. Use a spatula to spread the caramel glaze over the top of the rings. If desired, sprinkle edible pearls over the caramel glaze before it has set.

ACTUAL SIZE

Cookies

Cookies

Always delicious, homemade cookies in mini-morsel form are even more appealing, and they are easy to dress up for a special occasion. They are also relatively robust, making packaging and transporting worry free.

Vanilla Sugar Cookies

Having a recipe on hand for a cookie without a leavening agent is useful if you need to make tiny cookies. These vanilla sugar cookies hold their shape when baking.

Makes 45

1½ sticks (175 g) unsalted butter, softened
1 cup (200 g) superfine sugar
2 eggs
1 tsp vanilla extract
scant 3 cups (400 g) all-purpose flour, plus extra for dusting

Using an electric mixer, beat the butter and sugar together until light and creamy. Gradually beat in the eggs, one at a time, followed by the vanilla extract.

Sift in the flour and mix gently with a spoon until combined. Form the dough into a flattened disk, wrap in plastic wrap, and chill in the refrigerator for at least an hour until firm.

Preheat the oven to 350°F/180°C. Line a baking sheet with parchment paper. Let the dough soften slightly at room temperature, then roll it out on a lightly floured counter. Use cutters to cut out your desired shapes, then place them on the lined baking sheet. Bake the cookies in the preheated oven for 10–12 minutes, until the edges start to turn gold. Let cool completely on a wire rack before decorating.

TIPS

Chilling before baking helps softer doughs keep their shape and makes them easier to work with. The chilling time given is the optimum time for easy rolling and shaping. To speed up chilling, wrap the dough in plastic wrap and place in the freezer. About 20 minutes of chilling in the freezer is equal to 1 hour in the refrigerator.

Cookies should be baked on flat baking sheets lined with parchment paper, or on a silicone sheet. The baking sheet can have raised edges, but cookies will not brown evenly if the sheet is too deep.

A baking sheet should be cool or at room temperature when dough is placed on it, otherwise the dough will start to melt, which will affect the shape and texture of the cookie.

Make sure that all the cookies on one baking sheet are of a uniform thickness and size so they will bake in the same amount of time.

Let cookies cool before storing them; if they are still warm, they will "sweat" and become soggy.

FREEZING COOKIE DOUGH

Most unbaked cookie doughs freeze extremely well and can be kept frozen for up to 4–6 weeks. The most important thing to keep in mind is that the dough will absorb any odors present in your freezer if it's not properly wrapped and sealed, so wrap it twice securely in plastic wrap. When you are ready to bake, simply let the dough thaw in the refrigerator. This will take several hours, so plan ahead.

FREEZING BAKED COOKIES

Freezing baked, undecorated cookies is a great way to preserve their freshness; they will keep in the freezer for 3–4 weeks. Wrap twice securely in plastic wrap. When ready to eat them, let them come to room temperature, or put them in the microwave on high for about 30 seconds. (Times will differ, depending on the size of cookie.) Once thawed, the cookies can be iced.

Coffee Bean Cookies

Fragrant coffee shortbread is shaped into tiny oval cookies that look exactly like lightly roasted coffee beans, and they aren't a lot bigger—the characteristic line down the middle of each "bean" is marked using a toothpick. Put a handful into the saucer of each guest's cup of Java so that they can alternately crunch and sip.

To make 200

1½ sticks (175 g) unsalted
butter, softened

1 cup (200 g) superfine sugar

2 eggs

2 tsp espresso powder
or instant coffee granules

2 tbsp boiling water

½ tsp vanilla extract

scant 3 cups (400 g)
all-purpose flour

1 Using an electric mixer, beat the butter and sugar together until light and creamy. Gradually beat in the eggs, one at a time, until well combined. Mix the espresso powder or coffee granules with the boiling water to form a syrup. Add the coffee syrup and vanilla extract to the butter-and-sugar mixture and beat until smooth.

2 Sift in the flour, then mix gently with a spoon until well combined. Form the dough into a flattened disk, wrap it in plastic wrap, and chill in the refrigerator for at least an hour, until firm.

3 Preheat the oven to 350°F/180°C. Line two baking sheets with parchment paper. Let the dough soften slightly at room temperature. Roll small ovals of the cookie dough about ½ inch (1 cm) long and place them on the lined baking sheets. Press a toothpick horizontally along each cookie to imprint a line down the center to form the coffee bean shape. Bake the cookies in the preheated oven for 3–5 minutes, until just firm to the touch. Let them cool completely on a wire rack.

ACTUAL SIZE

Jewel Cookies

The royal icing that tops off these little gems sets hard, so they're a good choice if you need a treat that you can transport; they'll arrive looking neat and crisp. And with a range of different hues of pastel frosting, they make an exceptionally pretty plateful—perfect for everything from a reading-group coffee break to a kids' party favor.

To make 75

1¾ cups (250 g) all-purpose flour,
plus extra for dusting

½ tsp salt

½ tsp baking powder

2 tbsp superfine sugar

7 tbsp (100 g) unsalted butter,
softened and cubed

scant ⅔ cup (140 ml) milk

ROYAL ICING

scant 2¼ cups (250 g)
confectioners' sugar, sifted

1 extra-large egg white

½ tsp fresh lemon juice

assorted food colorings,
such as pink, purple,
orange, green

1 Mix all the dry ingredients together in a large bowl and then rub the butter into the mixture with your fingertips until it resembles coarse bread crumbs. Gradually mix in the milk with a spoon to bind the crumbs together and form a dough. Wrap the dough in plastic wrap and chill in the refrigerator for at least an hour, until firm.

2 Preheat the oven to 350°F/180°C. Line a large baking sheet with parchment paper. Roll out the dough on a lightly floured counter, then use a ¾-inch (2-cm) round cutter to cut out circles. Place them on the lined baking sheet and bake in the preheated oven for 20 minutes, or until they are lightly golden. Let the cookies cool completely on a wire rack before decorating.

3 To make the royal icing, use an electric mixer to mix the confectioners' sugar and egg white together on low speed for about 5 minutes, until the icing has a stiff-peak consistency. Mix in the lemon juice with a wooden spoon. Divide the icing into several bowls and add a small amount of a different food coloring to each one to create a variety of colors. Use a pastry bag fitted with a small star piping tip to pipe a small rosette of colored royal icing onto each cookie. Let the icing dry at room temperature (preferably overnight) before serving.

ACTUAL SIZE

Strawberry Sandwich Cookies

Crisp sugar cookies with a fruity filling; if you have any homemade strawberry preserve, it will elevate these into the luxury league, but even if you use a good-quality store-bought version, they will still taste pretty good. If you don't have a miniature cutter to make the hole in the center of the top cookie, you can use the end of a drinking straw.

1 Using an electric mixer, beat the butter and sugar together until light and creamy. Gradually beat in the eggs, one at a time, until well combined, followed by the vanilla extract.

2 Sift in the flour and mix gently with a spoon until well combined. Form the dough into a flattened disk, wrap it in plastic wrap, and chill in the refrigerator for at least an hour, until firm.

3 Preheat the oven to 350°F/180°C. Line a baking sheet with parchment paper. Let the dough soften slightly at room temperature. Roll out the dough on a lightly floured counter to about ¼ inch (5 mm) thick. Use a 1³⁄₈ -inch (3.5-cm) round cutter to cut out circles and place them on the lined baking sheet. Use a small star cutter (or another shape, if desired) to cut out a hole from the center in every second cookie. Bake the cookies in the preheated oven for 10–12 minutes, until the edges are lightly browned and the cookies are just firm to the touch. Let the cookies cool completely on a wire rack.

4 Spread strawberry preserve or jelly on each solid cookie, then press a cookie with a hole in it on top. If desired, dust with confectioners' sugar before serving.

To make 40

1½ sticks (175 g) unsalted
butter, softened

1 cup (200 g) superfine sugar

2 extra-large eggs

½ tsp vanilla extract

scant 3 cups (400 g) all-purpose flour,
plus extra for dusting

6 tbsp strawberry preserve or jelly

confectioners' sugar, for dusting
(optional)

ACTUAL SIZE

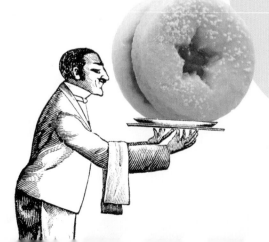

Tiered Cookie Towers

The brown sugar and cocoa powder in the cookie dough give these masterpieces a rich chocolaty edge, while the stacked construction makes them look like miniature wedding cakes, topped off with icing beads and pretty sugar roses. If you want to make them for an actual wedding, they could serve as elegant place-card props for the table settings, or as pretty favors for the guests.

To make 24

2 sticks (225 g) unsalted butter, softened

1 cup (225 g) firmly packed light brown sugar

1 extra-large egg, beaten

3 cups (425 g) all-purpose flour, plus extra for dusting

scant ⅓ cup (30 g) unsweetened cocoa powder

sugar roses or other edible decorations, for decorating

ROYAL ICING

scant 2¼ cups (250 g) confectioners' sugar, sifted

1 extra-large egg white

½ tsp fresh lemon juice

1 Using an electric mixer, beat the butter and sugar together until light and creamy. Gradually beat in the egg until well combined.

2 Sift in the flour and cocoa powder and mix on a slow speed until the ingredients start to clump together into a ball. Wrap the dough in plastic wrap and chill in the refrigerator for at least an hour, until firm.

3 Preheat the oven to 350°F/180°C. Line two baking sheets with parchment paper. Let the dough soften slightly at room temperature, then roll it out on a lightly floured counter until ¼ inch (5 mm) thick.

4 Use 1-inch (2.5-cm), 1⅜-inch (3.5-cm), and 1½-inch (4-cm) round cutters to cut out three different-size circles for each cookie. Place on the lined baking sheets and bake in the preheated oven for 10–12 minutes, until lightly browned and just firm to the touch. Let cool completely on a wire rack.

5 To make the royal icing, use an electric mixer to mix the confectioners' sugar and egg white together on low speed for about 5 minutes, until the icing has a stiff-peak consistency. Mix in the lemon juice with a wooden spoon. Use a small amount of royal icing to assemble each cookie tower with the smallest cookie on the top tier and the largest on the bottom tier so that the tower resembles a miniature three-tiered cake. Fill a pastry bag fitted with a ¼-inch (5-mm) round piping tip with the remaining royal icing and pipe small dots around the rim of each tier of each cookie tower. Top the towers with a sugar rose or another edible decoration, using royal icing to secure the decoration in place. Let the royal icing dry at room temperature (preferably overnight) before serving.

ACTUAL SIZE

Coconut Xs & Os

This chewy coconut mixture is simple to shape into anything you like—here they've been formed into miniature Xs and Os (play a game of tic-tac-toe and winner eats all ...), but you could just as easily make stars, flowers, butterflies, or any other simple shape. They're the quickest treats in the book to make, but they're baked at low heat, so they take a little extra time in the oven to cook.

1 Preheat the oven to 275°F/140°C. Line a baking sheet with parchment paper. Beat the egg whites in a clean, grease-free bowl until they form stiff peaks. Gently fold in the sugar and dry unsweetened coconut with a spatula until evenly combined. If desired, divide the dough into separate bowls and color the dough with different food colorings.

2 Let the dough stand for 15–20 minutes until firm, before shaping it into small X and O shapes. The dough can be shaped by hand, or it can be pressed inside small cutters (for this project I used an "O" and an "X" cutter from an alphabet set). Place the cookies on the lined baking sheet and bake in the preheated oven for 45 minutes, or until they just start to turn golden. Let the cookies cool completely on a wire rack before serving.

TIP Keep in mind that the color of the cookies, and any other tinted cookie dough, may darken when baked.

To make 30

2 extra-large egg whites

¾ cup (150 g) superfine sugar

1⅔ cups (150 g) dry unsweetened coconut

assorted food colorings, such as pink and purple (optional)

ACTUAL SIZE

Polka-Dot Lemon Shortbreads

Zesty lemon shortbread is topped with polka-dot icing, and each cookie is finished with a ribbon—these petites are almost (but not quite) too pretty to eat. The technique of "flooding" icing to add extra details is a useful one to have up your sleeve, especially for themed cookies; you can create any design you like to suit the occasion.

To make 45

1½ sticks (175 g) unsalted butter, softened

1 cup (200 g) superfine sugar

2 extra-large eggs

½ tsp vanilla extract

1 tsp limoncello or fresh lemon juice

scant 3 cups (400 g) all-purpose flour, plus extra for dusting

finely grated zest of ½ unwaxed lemon

ROYAL ICING

scant 2¼ cups (250 g) confectioners' sugar, sifted

1 extra-large egg white

½ tsp limoncello or fresh lemon juice

yellow food coloring

1 Using an electric mixer, beat the butter and sugar together until light and creamy. Gradually beat in the eggs, one at a time, followed by the vanilla extract and limoncello or lemon juice.

2 Sift in the flour and add the lemon zest, then mix gently with a spoon until well combined. Form the dough into a flattened disk, wrap it in plastic wrap, and chill in the refrigerator for at least an hour until firm.

3 Preheat the oven to 350°F/180°C. Line a baking sheet with parchment paper. Let the dough soften slightly at room temperature, then roll it out on a lightly floured counter until ¼ inch (5 mm) thick. Use a 1½-inch (4-cm) round cutter to cut out circles. Place the circles on the lined baking sheet and then use the end of a round piping tip to cut out a little hole in the side of each cookie. Bake in the preheated oven for 10–12 minutes, until the edges start to turn gold. Let the cookies cool completely on a wire rack.

4 To make the royal icing, use an electric mixer to mix the confectioners' sugar and egg white together on low speed for about 5 minutes, until the icing has a stiff-peak consistency. Mix in the limoncello or lemon juice with a wooden spoon. Fill a pastry bag fitted with a small round piping tube with one-third of the royal icing. Pipe around the edge of each cookie and around the edge of the small hole in each cookie. Spoon half the remaining icing into a bowl and color it with yellow food coloring. Slowly stir a few drops of water into the icing until it is a runny consistency. Add a few drops of water to the remaining white icing until it is also a runny consistency. Fill two squeeze bottles with the runny icings. Gently squeeze the white icing into the outlined section of each cookie to "flood" it until the icing covers all of the surface. While the icing is still wet, squeeze small drops of the yellow icing onto the flooded surface to create a polka-dot pattern. Let the cookies dry at room temperature (preferably overnight), then tie a thin ribbon bow through each hole.

ACTUAL SIZE

TIP Let the cookies dry under a lamp to achieve a shiny surface.

Cupcakes

Cupcakes

There are oodles of cupcake recipes in books and online, but it's harder to find as many recipes for their miniature friends. Fortunately, it is not difficult to downsize your favorite cupcake recipes with a few simple tips.

MAKING MINI CUPCAKES

Most cupcake recipes can be used to make mini cupcakes. Mini cupcake baking pans hold about one-third of the amount of regular cupcake baking pans, so if you have a recipe that yields 12 full-size cupcakes, you'll get about 36 minis from the same amount of batter. It is much easier to start with the full recipe and make a big batch of miniature cupcakes than to reduce the quantities of the ingredients in the recipe.

Once you have made your cupcake batter, line the mini cupcake pan sections with mini paper cupcake liners and add batter to each one until they are two-thirds full. It is often difficult and time-consuming to use a teaspoon to scoop the batter into the liners, so to save time, fill a large disposable pastry bag fitted with a small round piping tip with the cupcake batter and pipe the batter into the liners. Piping the batter will also help to make sure that the cupcakes are approximately the same size.

BAKING TIMES FOR MINI CUPCAKES

While most regular cupcakes take about 20–25 minutes to bake, miniature cupcakes bake in a shorter period of time, and on average need only 10–15 minutes until they are done. After 10 minutes of baking time, it is useful to insert a toothpick into one of the cupcakes to see if they are baked all the way through. If the toothpick doesn't come out clean when withdrawn from the cupcake, return the cupcakes to the oven for a few more minutes.

It's easy to overbake miniature cupcakes, so be sure to keep a close eye on them while they are baking in the oven.

ADDING INGREDIENTS TO MINI CUPCAKES

If your regular cupcake recipe calls for ingredients such as fruit, nuts, or chocolate chips to be stirred into the batter, it is important to be mindful that unless these ingredients are chopped finely, they can overwhelm the miniature cupcakes. While whole blueberries are a nice surprise in a regular-size cupcake, they can take up most of the space in a mini cupcake liner, leaving little room for the batter. Remember to always scale down your extra ingredients so that they are proportional to the size of the miniature cupcakes.

DECORATING MINI CUPCAKES

It is also easy to make a miniature cupcake look too top-heavy. Decorating with small toppings works best, such as sprinkles, crushed nuts, and small chocolates, instead of whole fruit or large fondant toppers.

If you intend to display your cupcakes on a cake stand or on a plate, it is easiest to pipe frosting on top of them and add any other decorations once the display has been arranged. Reducing the amount of times you need to pick up and move the cupcakes will help to make sure that the frosting is not smudged. Cupcakes should be frosted on the day they are to be served.

STORING CUPCAKES

Cupcakes can be stored overnight in a cupcake box at room temperature. Cupcakes with perishable frostings should ideally be eaten the same day, or refrigerated and consumed the following day. Undecorated cupcakes can be frozen after baking. Bring them to room temperature when you're ready to decorate them.

Peanut Butter Chocolate Cupcakes

Every treat list needs a chocolate cupcake, and this is mine—dark chocolate and brown sugar combine to give the mix a great flavor, while ground almonds keep the sponge light and moist. The cakes are finished with rosettes of peanut butter frosting—a natural pairing with the rich cake, and one that balances the chocolate beautifully.

To make 30

2¼ oz (60 g) semisweet chocolate, chopped

scant ¾ cup (160 ml) water

7 tbsp (100 g) unsalted butter, softened

generous 1 cup (225 g) firmly packed dark brown sugar

2 extra-large eggs

scant ¾ cup (100 g) all-purpose flour

¾ tsp baking powder

2 tbsp unsweetened cocoa powder

½ cup (40 g) almond flour

PEANUT BUTTER FROSTING

3½ tbsp (50 g) unsalted butter, softened

generous ⅓ cup (100 g) smooth peanut butter

scant 2⅔ cups (300 g) confectioners' sugar, sifted

scant ¼ cup (50 ml) milk

2 tbsp salted roasted peanuts

1 Preheat the oven to 350°F/180°C. Line 30 sections of mini cupcake baking pans with mini paper cupcake liners. To make the cupcakes, stir the chocolate and water together in a small saucepan over low heat until smooth. Using an electric mixer, beat the butter, sugar, and eggs together until light and fluffy. Stir the flour, baking powder, cocoa powder, almond flour, and warm chocolate into the mixture until well combined.

2 Spoon the batter into the cupcake liners until they are half full and bake in the preheated oven for about 15 minutes, or until a toothpick inserted into the center of a cupcake comes out clean. Let the cupcakes cool for a few minutes in the baking pan before turning them out onto a wire rack to cool completely.

3 For the peanut butter frosting, use an electric mixer to beat the butter and peanut butter together on a high speed for about 2 minutes, until light and fluffy, then gradually beat in the sugar and milk until light and smooth. Fill a pastry bag fitted with a small star piping tip with the frosting and pipe a small rosette of frosting onto each cupcake. Top with half a peanut to finish.

ACTUAL SIZE

White Russian Cupcakes

Based on the classic cocktail that's traditionally made with vodka, coffee liqueur, and cream, these innocent-looking minis are much less potent but just as delicious as the drink that inspired them. If you want an alcohol-free version, replace the coffee liqueur and vodka with a little coffee flavoring—your cupcakes will taste just as good.

To make 24

scant 1 cup (125 g) all-purpose flour

½ tsp baking powder

¼ tsp baking soda

small pinch of salt

5 tbsp Kahlúa, or to taste

2 tsp instant coffee granules

1 stick (115 g) unsalted butter, softened

scant 1 cup (175 g) superfine sugar

2 extra-large egg whites

5 tbsp lowfat milk

small sugar flowers, for decorating (optional)

WHITE CHOCOLATE VODKA GANACHE

⅔ cup (150 ml) heavy cream

2 tbsp (25 g) unsalted butter

9 oz (250 g) white chocolate, melted (*see page 41*)

6 tbsp vodka

KAHLÚA SWISS MERINGUE BUTTERCREAM

scant ⅔ cup (120 g) superfine sugar

2 extra-large egg whites

2 sticks plus 1 tbsp (240 g) unsalted butter, softened

6 tbsp Kahlúa, or to taste

1 Preheat the oven to 350°F/180°C. Line a 24-section mini muffin baking pan with mini paper cupcake liners. Mix the flour, baking powder, baking soda, and salt together in a bowl and set aside. In a separate bowl, whisk together the Kahlúa and coffee granules. Using an electric mixer, beat the butter and sugar together until light and fluffy. Add the egg whites, one at a time, and mix until well combined. Alternate adding the milk, flour mixture, and Kahlúa mixture to the cake batter and beat until combined.

2 Spoon the cake batter into the cupcake liners until they are two-thirds full, then bake in the preheated oven for about 12 minutes, or until a toothpick inserted into the center of a cupcake comes out clean. Turn out the cupcakes onto a wire rack to cool completely before filling and decorating.

3 While the cupcakes are baking, make the ganache. Heat the cream and butter in a small saucepan until small bubbles appear, then remove the pan from the heat and add the melted white chocolate. Stir until completely combined and smooth, then stir in the vodka. Cover and chill the ganache in the refrigerator for about an hour.

4 For the buttercream, add the sugar to the egg whites in a heatproof bowl set over a small saucepan of simmering water and whisk until the sugar dissolves completely. Remove the bowl from the pan and use an electric mixer to beat the mixture on a high speed for about 5 minutes, until it is bright white in color and does not move in the bowl. Divide the butter into eight blocks. Reduce the mixer speed to medium and add the butter, one block at a time, then mix in the Kahlúa. Place the buttercream in a pastry bag fitted with a small star piping tip.

5 Use a small knife or a cupcake corer to remove the top two-thirds of the core from the center of each cupcake, then fill with the ganache. Pipe a buttercream swirl on top of each cupcake and, if desired, add a small sugar flower to finish.

ACTUAL SIZE

Mojito Cupcakes

The pleasure of a great mojito lies in the balance of its flavors; rum, lime, and mint all need to be in harmony for the drink to taste good. These mini mojitos are all you could want in a cocktail—but in a cupcake. Once baked, the little cakes are soaked in a rum and mint syrup before being topped with a swirl of lime buttercream, with a touch more rum. Intoxicating, delicious, and the perfect mini-dessert for a special dinner.

1 Preheat the oven to 350°F/180°C. Line two 24-section mini cupcake baking pans with mini paper cupcake liners. To make the cupcakes, mix the flour, baking powder, baking soda, and salt together in a bowl and set aside. In a separate bowl, whisk together the buttermilk, rum, and vanilla extract. Using an electric mixer, beat the butter and sugar together for about 5 minutes, until light and fluffy. Add the eggs, one at a time, and mix until well combined. Alternate adding the flour mixture and buttermilk mixture to the cake batter and beat until combined.

2 Spoon the batter into the cupcake liners until they are two-thirds full, then bake in the preheated oven for 12–15 minutes, or until a toothpick inserted into the center of a cupcake comes out clean. Turn out the cupcakes onto a wire rack to cool for a few minutes.

3 While the cupcakes are baking and cooling slightly, make the rum syrup. Place the butter, sugar, and water in a saucepan and bring to a boil, stirring often until the butter has completely melted and the sugar has dissolved. Remove the pan from the heat and carefully add the rum; the mixture will bubble, so be careful not to burn yourself. Add the lime zest and juice and mint, then let the syrup infuse for 5 minutes before removing the mint leaves.

4 Use a toothpick to poke holes all over the tops of the warm cupcakes, then immediately spoon over the rum syrup and let them soak it up. Let the cupcakes cool completely before frosting them.

5 For the buttercream, use an electric mixer to beat the butter on high speed for about 2 minutes until light and fluffy, then gradually beat in the sugar (about 1¾ cups at a time) on low speed. Once all the sugar is incorporated, increase the speed to high again and mix for another 2–3 minutes. Add the rum and lime juice and mix on medium speed until well incorporated. Place the buttercream in a pastry bag fitted with a small star piping tip and pipe a swirl onto each cupcake. Sprinkle lime zest on top to finish.

To make 48

2⅔ cups (375 g) all-purpose flour
1 tsp baking powder
½ tsp baking soda
pinch of salt
generous 1 cup (275 ml) buttermilk
1 tbsp dark rum
½ tsp vanilla extract
2 sticks (225 g) unsalted butter, softened
2¼ cups (450 g) superfine sugar
4 large eggs

RUM SYRUP

4 tbsp (55 g) unsalted butter
generous 1 cup (225 g) superfine sugar
4 tbsp cold water
4 tbsp dark rum
finely grated zest and juice of ½ unwaxed lime
½ cup (25 g) fresh mint leaves

LIME & RUM BUTTERCREAM

2 sticks plus 1 tbsp (240 g) unsalted butter, softened
scant 5¼ cups (600 g) confectioners' sugar, sifted
4 tbsp dark rum
juice of 1 unwaxed lime, and finely grated zest, to decorate

ACTUAL SIZE

White Chocolate Mudcakes

Mudcakes are usually made with dark chocolate, but these little cupcakes are the vanilla versions, flavored with creamy white chocolate and topped off with a two-tone swirl of raspberry-vanilla buttercream and sugar heart confetti—making them perfect little treats for Valentine's Day or an anniversary.

To make 48

9 tbsp (125 g) unsalted butter, softened and chopped

3 oz (80 g) white chocolate

1 cup (225 g) superfine sugar

½ cup (125 ml) milk

1 cup (150 g) all-purpose flour

½ tsp baking powder

1 extra-large egg

sprinkles, such as mini pink hearts, for decorating

BUTTERCREAM

1½ sticks (175 g) unsalted butter, softened

3 cups (350 g) confectioners' sugar, sifted

1 tsp vanilla extract

2 tbsp cooled boiled water

2 tbsp raspberry preserve or jelly

1 Preheat the oven to 350°F/180°C. Line two 24-section mini cupcake baking pans with mini paper cupcake liners. Stir the butter, white chocolate, sugar, and milk together in a small saucepan over low heat until smooth. Transfer to a medium bowl and let cool to room temperature.

2 Beat the flour and baking powder into the cooled mixture, then beat in the egg. Spoon the batter into the cupcake liners until they are two-thirds full, then bake in the preheated oven for about 15 minutes, or until a toothpick inserted into the center of a cupcake comes out clean. Let the cupcakes cool for a few minutes in the pan before turning them out onto a wire rack to cool completely.

3 To make the buttercream, use an electric mixer to beat the butter and confectioners' sugar together on high speed for about 5 minutes until light and fluffy. Add the vanilla extract and water, then mix on medium speed until well incorporated. Divide the mixture between two bowls. Stir the raspberry preserve or jelly through one bowl of buttercream and leave the other bowl plain. Fill one side of a pastry bag fitted with a small star piping tip with the vanilla buttercream and the other side with the raspberry buttercream. Squeeze the buttercream out of the bag and into a bowl until you achieve a two-toned effect. Pipe a two-toned swirl of buttercream onto each cupcake, and top with sprinkles, such as mini pink sugar hearts, to finish.

TIP Add any sprinkles or decorations while the buttercream is still fresh otherwise they won't stick in place.

ACTUAL SIZE

Coconut Cupcakes

These little layered beauties will charm anyone that has a sweet tooth. A fluffy vanilla interior is given a strawberry and whipped cream filling, coated with a pink icing and, as a final touch, rolled in dry unsweetened coconut—a wonderful range of flavors squeezed into a bite-size cupcake.

To make 36

generous 1 cup (150 g)
all-purpose flour

1 tsp baking powder

7 tbsp (100 g) unsalted butter,
softened

1 tsp vanilla extract

½ cup (115 g) superfine sugar

2 extra-large eggs

2 tbsp milk

ICING & TOPPING

1 cup (115 g) confectioners' sugar

½ tsp unsalted butter

2 drops of pink food coloring

1 tbsp hot water

generous ¾ cup (75 g) dry
unsweetened coconut

10 tbsp strawberry preserve or jelly

1¼ cups (300 ml) heavy cream,
whipped until it holds its shape

sugar flowers, for decorating
(optional)

1 Preheat the oven to 350°F/180°C. Line 36 sections of mini cupcake baking pans with mini paper cupcake liners. Sift the flour and baking powder into a bowl, then add the butter, vanilla extract, sugar, eggs, and milk. Using an electric mixer, beat the ingredients together on low speed until well combined. Increase the mixing speed to medium, then beat until the mixture becomes pale.

2 Spoon the cake batter into the cupcake liners until they are half full, then bake in the preheated oven for about 12 minutes, or until a toothpick inserted into the center of a cupcake comes out clean. Turn out the cupcakes onto a wire rack to cool completely.

3 To make the icing, sift the sugar into a small heatproof bowl and stir in the butter, pink food coloring, and hot water to make a thick paste. Place the bowl over a small saucepan of simmering water and stir until the icing reaches a spreadable consistency.

4 Once the cupcakes have cooled, use a spatula to spread the icing on the top of each cupcake, then immediately dip them into the dry unsweetened coconut. Let the icing set for a few minutes, then use a small knife to carefully cut a hole in the top of each cupcake. Fill each hole two-thirds full with strawberry preserve or jelly. Place the whipped cream in a pastry bag fitted with a small star piping tip and pipe a swirl of cream on top of each filled hole. If desired, add a sugar flower on top to finish.

ACTUAL SIZE

Savory

Savory

Cute bakes don't have to be limited to desserts. They say the best things come in small packages, and it's no exception when it comes to flavor-packed, bite-size canapés. Traditionally, canapés have a base made from puff pastry or cookie, which can support any number or combination of toppings.

Puff Pastry Dough

Making puff pastry dough takes time and effort, so the recipes in this book recommend that you use store-bought puff pastry. However, if time is on your side and you want to make your own puff pastry, here's a recipe you can try:

1¾ cups (250 g) all-purpose flour, plus extra for dusting
½ tsp salt
3 tbsp (40 g) unsalted butter, chilled and cubed
½ cup (125 ml) iced water
7 tbsp (100 g) unsalted butter, softened

Place the flour and salt in a large bowl and add the cubes of chilled butter.

Use your fingertips to rub the butter into the flour until the mixture resembles fine bread crumbs. Make a well in the center of the mixture and pour in the iced water. Mix the ingredients together until well combined. Form the mixture into a ball, wrap it in plastic wrap, and chill in the refrigerator for 30 minutes.

Use a lightly floured rolling pin to roll out the dough into a 4-inch x 12-inch (10-cm x 30-cm) rectangle. Place the softened butter between two sheets of plastic wrap and tap with a rolling pin to make a 3¼-inch x 3½-inch (8-cm x 9-cm) rectangle. Lay the dough on a lightly floured counter with a short edge closest to you. Remove the plastic wrap from the butter and place it in the center of the dough. Fold the end closest to you over the butter, then fold the opposite end over the top so that the butter is enclosed in the dough.

Turn the dough 90 degrees clockwise and gently press the edges together. Use a lightly floured nonstick rolling pin to gently tap the dough to flatten the butter. Roll out the dough to a 4-inch x 12-inch (10-cm x 30-cm) rectangle and repeat the folding process as before. Cover the dough with plastic wrap and place in the refrigerator for 30 minutes to rest.

Remove the dough from the refrigerator and repeat the rolling and folding process two more times. Cover with plastic wrap and place in the refrigerator for 30 minutes to rest. Repeat the rolling and folding process an additional two times and then place in the refrigerator for 30 minutes to rest. (The dough should have been folded and rolled six times altogether.)

Remove the dough from the refrigerator, unwrap and give it a final two rolls and folds before rolling it out to the size required for your chosen recipe.

TIPS

Canapés should be no bigger than one bite or else you are risking entering the realm of finger food.

Fresh, in-season ingredients will always lead you to the most beautiful tasting canapés.

Often, canapés need building at the last minute, so have all the components ready in advance to make assembly quick and easy. It's also a good idea to have a clear vision of what the finished canapés will look like well in advance so that you can quickly plate them up and serve them once the guests arrive, instead of fussing about with finishing touches.

Spinach & Feta Triangles

Inspired by the Greek *spanakopita* but encased in puff pastry instead of the more traditional phyllo, these walnut-size snacks are airy and light, with a crunchy outside and a cheesy spinach filling warmed with a hint of nutmeg. Served warm, they're the perfect finger food, which means they'll disappear quickly, so consider baking a double batch.

To make 40

5 cups (250 g) baby spinach leaves, chopped

2 scallions, thinly sliced

3½ oz (100 g) feta cheese, coarsely chopped

finely grated zest of ½ unwaxed lemon

¼ tsp ground nutmeg

12-inch x 7½-inch (30-cm x 19-cm) piece of ready-to-bake puff pastry, just thawed if frozen

all-purpose flour, for dusting

1 large egg, beaten

salt and freshly ground black pepper

1 Preheat the oven to 400°F/200°C. Line two baking sheets with parchment paper. Bring a saucepan of salted water to a boil, add the spinach and scallions, and blanch for 1 minute. Drain well, squeezing out any excess water, and place in a bowl. Add the feta, lemon zest, and nutmeg, season to taste with salt and black pepper, and mix well.

2 Lay the puff pastry on a floured counter and use a 1½-inch (4-cm) square cutter to cut out 40 squares. Divide the filling among the pastry squares, then brush the edges with the beaten egg. Fold the pastry in half diagonally to enclose the filling and make a triangle. Pinch the edges to seal.

3 Place the triangles on the lined baking sheets, then brush the tops with beaten egg. Bake in the preheated oven for 15 minutes, or until puffed and golden. Serve warm.

ACTUAL SIZE

Caesar Salad Bites

This classic salad makes a good party snack when it's reduced to miniature form. Garlic butter-infused bread is baked until golden to make a croutonlike tart to contain finely shredded lettuce, crispy bacon, and Parmesan cheese. Quail egg halves complete the picture. Pretty to look at and gorgeous to eat.

To make 24

butter, for greasing

10 slices of white bread

7 tbsp (100 g) garlic butter
(or plain butter if you prefer), melted

1 tbsp vegetable or olive oil

3 bacon slices, cut
into thin slices

12 quail eggs

1 Boston lettuce

scant ¼ cup (25 g) finely grated
Parmesan cheese

CAESAR SALAD
DRESSING

1 garlic clove

2 anchovy fillets in oil,
drained

5 tbsp mayonnaise

1 tbsp white wine vinegar

grating of Parmesan cheese

salt and freshly ground black pepper

1 Preheat the oven to 325°F/160°C. Grease the sections of a 24-section mini muffin baking pan. Remove the crusts from the slices of bread. Use a 1½-inch (4-cm) round cutter to cut out circles from the bread, then brush them with the melted garlic butter and press into the greased sections of the baking pan. Bake in the preheated oven for 10 minutes, or until golden. Heat the oil in a skillet and cook the bacon slices until crispy. Place them on paper towels to drain and cool.

2 To make the Caesar salad dressing, peel the garlic clove and crush it finely using a garlic crusher into a small bowl. Add the anchovies and use a fork to mash them to a paste. Add the mayonnaise, vinegar, and Parmesan cheese, and stir it all together. Season to taste with salt and black pepper. If the dressing is too thick, thin it down with a few teaspoons of water.

3 To softly boil the quail eggs, place them in a saucepan and cover with cold water. Bring to a boil, then immediately remove from the heat. Cool the eggs under cold running water, then carefully peel and cut in half.

4 To assemble the salads, finely shred the lettuce and top with the Caesar salad dressing. Fill the bread tartlet shells with the lettuce, then add a little Parmesan cheese and a sprinkling of crispy bacon pieces. Place a quail egg half on the top of each salad to finish.

ACTUAL SIZE

Pesto Pinwheels

Pinwheels, redolent of paper windmill toys and spinning fireworks, instantly create a festive feel. These spicy pastry versions are superfast to put together—the different ingredients can be bought already prepared, and with some neat assembly, you're only half an hour away from a sophisticated-looking canapé.

1 Preheat the oven to 350°F/180°C. Line a baking sheet with parchment paper. Roll out the puff pastry on a floured counter until about $^1/_{16}$ inch (2 mm) thick. Use a 1½-inch (4-cm) square cutter to cut out squares of pastry. For each square, use a small knife to make a cut diagonally from each corner of the square to ½ inch (1 cm) from the center to create four segments. Lightly brush the edge of each segment with milk.

2 Spoon a small dollop of pesto into the center of each square and then, starting at the top right-hand corner, work clockwise around the square and fold one corner of each segment toward the center to conceal the pesto and create the pinwheel shape.

3 Place the tomato paste in a pastry bag fitted with a small round piping tip. Brush the surface of the pastry with milk, then pipe a small dab of tomato paste in the center of each pinwheel. Sprinkle dried oregano over the pinwheels and place them on the lined baking sheet, then bake them in the preheated oven for about 10 minutes, or until they are golden brown and crisp. Serve them warm or cold.

To make 50

7-oz (200-g) block of puff pastry, thawed if frozen

all-purpose flour, for dusting

2 tbsp milk

4 tbsp pesto

5 tbsp tomato paste

dried oregano, for sprinkling

ACTUAL SIZE

Mini Blini Stacks with Smoked Salmon

Blinis are Russian pancakes, traditionally made with buckwheat and served with caviar. My versions are a little lighter (I used all-purpose flour) and much more purse-friendly (smoked salmon replaces the caviar), but they taste just as good. The blinis should be cool before you assemble the stacks, making them a versatile canapé base.

To make 30

generous 1 cup (150 g)
all-purpose flour

1 tbsp superfine sugar

3 tsp baking powder

pinch of salt

generous ¾ cup milk

1 extra-large egg

3½ tbsp (50 g) unsalted butter,
melted and cooled

9 oz (250 g) smoked salmon,
cut into small strips

⅔ cup (150 g) crème fraîche
or Greek yogurt

2 tbsp finely chopped fresh chives

1 Sift the flour, sugar, baking powder, and salt into a large bowl. Gradually beat in the milk and egg, then half the melted butter. Cover and chill the batter in the refrigerator for 30 minutes. When the batter is ready to use, spoon it into a squeeze bottle.*

2 Heat a large skillet over medium-high heat and lightly brush the skillet with a little of the remaining butter. Squeeze small circles, about 1 inch (2.5 cm) in diameter, of the blini batter into the skillet. Cook for about 30 seconds, or until browned lightly underneath and bubbles begin to appear on the surface. Use a spatula to gently turn the blinis over, then cook the other side for an additional 30 seconds, until brown. Repeat with the remaining blini batter to create at least 90 mini blinis.

3 To serve, stack three blinis on top of each other, with the smoked salmon and some of the crème fraîche or Greek yogurt sandwiched in between the bottom two layers. Top each stack with the remaining crème fraîche or yogurt and a sprinkling of chives. Keep the blini stacks refrigerated until ready to serve.

ACTUAL SIZE

*NOTE A squeeze bottle will help control the size of the blinis, because it will allow for the batter to be gradually squeezed into the skillet until the desired size is reached. If you don't have a squeeze bottle, just use a teaspoon to transfer the batter to the skillet.

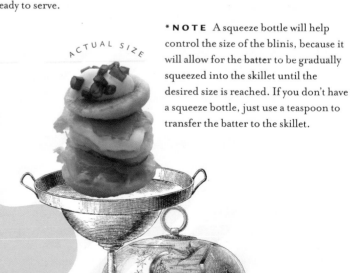

Caramelized Onion Galettes with Goat Cheese

Take your time softening the onion for these little puff pastry galettes—helped along by the wine and brown sugar, they'll take on a delicious savory-sweet flavor that's beautifully offset by the tangy goat cheese and a few thyme leaves, carefully picked so there are no rogue pieces of stem to ruin the texture.

To make 45

1 tbsp olive oil

1 brown onion, thinly sliced

1 tbsp packed light brown sugar

5 tbsp red wine

13 oz (375 g) ready-to-bake puff pastry, just thawed if frozen

all-purpose flour, for dusting

egg wash (1 extra-large egg beaten with 1 tbsp cold water)

2¾ oz (75 g) goat cheese, cut into small slices

3 tsp fresh thyme leaves, plus extra sprigs (optional) for garnishing

salt and freshly ground black pepper

1 Preheat the oven to 350°F/180°C. Line two baking sheets with parchment paper. Heat the oil in a saucepan and sauté the onion over low heat until softened. Add the sugar and cook for an additional 5 minutes. Add the red wine and salt and black pepper to taste and simmer the onion, stirring regularly, for about 5 minutes, until sticky and caramelized.

2 Place the puff pastry sheet on a floured counter and use a 1¼-inch (3-cm) round cutter to cut out 45 circles of pastry. Use a smaller round cutter, about 1-inch (2.5-cm) in diameter, to score a circle inside each pastry circle to create a small rim. Place the circles, evenly spaced, on the lined baking sheets. Brush the rim of each pastry circle lightly with egg wash, then bake in the preheated oven for 10 minutes.

3 Remove the galettes from the oven and use the back of a teaspoon to press down the inner circles so that they drop down, or come away. Fill each pastry shell with the caramelized onion, then top with a small slice of goat cheese. Sprinkle the thyme leaves over the galettes, then return them to the oven to bake for an additional 10 minutes. If desired, add extra thyme sprigs on top to garnish before serving warm or cold.

ACTUAL SIZE

Choux Buns with Blue Cheese Mousse

Although you may have a mental picture of cream puffs smothered in sweet chocolate sauce, the savory version tastes terrific, too. A rich, chive-dotted blue cheese filling is piped into the choux buns to create the ultimate cocktail party canapé.

To make 60

½ quantity of Choux Pastry
(*see page 69*)

BLUE CHEESE MOUSSE

6 oz (175 g) soft blue cheese
½ cup (115 g) cream cheese
5 tbsp heavy cream
½ bunch of fresh chives,
finely chopped, plus extra
for sprinkling (optional)
salt and freshly ground
black pepper

1 Preheat the oven to 425°F/220°C. Line two baking sheets with parchment paper. Spoon the choux pastry into a pastry bag fitted with a ¼-inch (5-mm) round piping tip. Pipe sixty small balls of the pastry about ¾ inch (2 cm) in diameter, evenly spaced, onto the lined baking sheets. Use a damp pastry brush to smooth the top of each ball if they have peaks before baking them in the preheated oven for 10 minutes. Reduce the oven temperature to 350°F/180°C, then bake for an additional 5 minutes, or until the choux balls are crisp. Make a small slit in the base of each ball to release the steam, then let cool completely on the baking sheets.

2 To make the blue cheese mousse, blend the blue cheese and cream cheese together in a food processor or in a bowl with a handheld electric mixer until completely smooth. Season to taste with salt and black pepper. In a separate bowl, whip the cream until soft peaks form. Fold the whipped cream into the blue cheese mixture and stir until the mixture is creamy, then fold in the finely chopped chives.

3 To fill the buns, transfer the mousse into a pastry bag fitted with a ⅛-inch (2.5-mm) round piping tip. Insert the tip into the slit in the bottom of the bun and gently squeeze the pastry bag so that the mousse fills the cavity of the bun. A little mousse will come back out of the hole if the bun is completely filled. Repeat until all the choux buns are filled. Serve sprinkled with chopped chives, if desired.

ACTUAL SIZE

Cheese-Straw Bundles with Paprika

Tiny bundles of cheese straws laced with paprika for a hint of smoky heat, then tied together with fresh chives—this is a great use for leftover puff pastry. And mildly fussy chive-tying apart, these are quick to make, too. Serve with a glass of something sparkling.

To make 50 bundles

7-oz (200-g) block of puff pastry, thawed if frozen

all-purpose flour, for dusting

scant 1 cup (100 g) finely grated Gruyère cheese

1 tbsp sweet smoked paprika

1 medium egg, beaten

2 tbsp freshly grated Parmesan cheese

1 bunch of fresh chives

1 Roll out the puff pastry on a floured counter until about ⅝ inch (1.5 cm) thick. Spread one-third of the Gruyère cheese and one-third of the smoked paprika evenly over the surface of the pastry, then use a nonstick rolling pin to roll the ingredients firmly into the pastry.

2 Fold the pastry in half and roll it out again until about ⅝ inch (1.5 cm) thick. Repeat the process twice more with the remaining thirds of the Gruyère and paprika, then roll out the pastry into a 11-inch x 7-inch (28-cm x 18-cm) rectangle about 1/16 inch (2 mm) thick. Brush the pastry with the beaten egg and sprinkle the Parmesan cheese over it. Let the pastry rest in the refrigerator for 30 minutes. Meanwhile, preheat the oven to 350°F/180°C. Line a large baking sheet with parchment paper.

3 Cut the pastry into tiny strips about 1½ inches (4 cm) long and ⅛ inch (3 mm) wide. Carefully take each strip of pastry and twist each end in opposite directions until the whole strip is evenly twisted, then lay them on the lined baking sheet. Bake the cheese straws in the preheated oven for about 5 minutes, or until they are golden brown and crisp. Let them cool completely on the baking sheet.

4 To serve, group four or five of the cheese straws together into small bundles and tie them together with the chives.

ACTUAL SIZE

Index

About the author

Fiona Pearce started cake decorating and food styling as a hobby in 2009 when she moved to London from Sydney. Inspired by the vintage era, she started her blog Icing Bliss (www.icingbliss.blogspot.com), where she records her adventures baking and trawling through rummage sales collecting vintage treasures. She also posts online tutorials to show readers how to make vintage-inspired bakes and craft projects.

Fiona teaches cake-decorating classes in southwest London, and has written and contributed to a number of baking and craft books and magazines. This is her second book.

Acknowledgments

Many thanks to everyone at Ivy Press, in particular to my editor Tom Kitch and to Wayne Blades and Simon Daley for the lovely design. A huge thank you to my project editor Jo Richardson, and to my wonderful photographer Sian Irvine and her assistant Joe Giacomet, who worked incredibly hard to capture the treats in their best light. Much love to all my wonderful friends and family for their support, and extra special thanks to my husband Dave for turning a blind eye to all the mess in the kitchen for months as I tested recipes, and for loving me through it all.

Ivy Press would like to thank:

Cheese Please
www.cheesepleaseonline.co.uk

Steamer Trading Cookshop
www.steamer.co.uk

Flint
www.flintcollection.com